DYNAMICS OF
SPIRITUAL
DECEPTION

DYNAMICS OF SPIRITUAL DECEPTION

Daniel C. Juster

Destiny Image Publishers
P.O. Box 310
Shippensburg, PA 17257

"Speaking to the Purposes of God
for this Generation"

ISBN 1-56043-120-2

For Worldwide Distribution
Printed in the U.S.A.

Destiny Image books are available through these fine distributors outside the United States:

Christian Growth, Inc.
Jalan Kilang-Timor, Singapore 0315

Lifestream
Nottingham, England

Rhema Ministries Trading
Randburg, South Africa

Salvation Book Centre
Petaling, Jaya, Malaysia

Successful Christian Living
Capetown, Rep. of South Africa

Vision Resources
Ponsonby, Auckland, New Zealand

WA Buchanan Company
Geebung, Queensland, Australia

Word Alive
Niverville, Manitoba, Canada

DEDICATION

To the late Chaplain Dr. Evan D. Welsh and Mrs. Evan (Oleina May) Welsh. Their spiritual life and love gave an image of truth which kept us during difficult years.

PREFACE

Twenty-four years ago my wife and I were part of a church that fell into depths of spiritual deception and became cultic. The events of those days led to the ruin of many lives. Most shocking of all was the number of students from Evangelical backgrounds who were so easily deceived. How did this happen? What were the spiritual principles involved which led to such great tragedy?

It is my conviction that the account of this congregation and the principles involved in their deception will prevent the same thing from occurring elsewhere. May those who read this learn to guard themselves against the dynamics of spiritual deception.

Due to the sensitive nature of this story, names and places have been altered. However the substance of this account is true.

The
Story of
Deception

I. THE STORY OF DECEPTION

We sat in a circle, sang lively choruses and clapped our hands. Then we stood in reverence and sang worship choruses. The words were sung with great feeling and awe:

"Bless the Lord, oh my soul and all that is within me bless His holy name."

Some eyes were closed, others reflected the presence of tears. Hands were raised in adoration, and as the chorus came to an end, many began to sing in hushed tones of strange syllables. It was a peculiar harmony, like that of an aeolian harp, and it had an eerie beauty. This was followed by silence, until one man across this circle of 25 to 35 people began to speak out aloud in strange syllables:

"Shobo-to ka a be, shodo-ma son-danai, kobakai lodo-ma kambi, shoto-ma kandi, tobatai shobo-to kabe, kobakai, sundakai."*

---

*Although this is not the exact speech, it is a reasonable approximation of the sound from this man, heard many times over two years.

Silence followed, Than an attractive short-haired girl whom I had not yet met said, "I love you, my people. Abide in me forever. I love you and give you life."

Then others spoke. Some read Scripture. Others gave words as if God were speaking through them in the first person:

"My children, I desire to dwell in your midst. Yield yourselves wholly to me, then I will fill you. You cannot do it, but only by my living my life through you. Thus saith the Lord."

Several others spoke in a similar vein. My mind was racing, why did so many speak in King James Elizabethan English? Was this really the Word of the Lord? Were these the gifts of the Spirit? Was I in the midst of the supernatural presence of God? Was this group returning to a real New Testament expression of the power and presence of God?

But the biggest question of all was, what was I doing at the Sheepfold Church? This was not my first experience with "Charismatics" or "Pentacostal Christians." Nor was I ignorant of their doctrine. I began to look back over my life to discover what had led me there.

Because my father was Jewish and my mother a Norwegian Christian, I was not raised in either a church or a synagogue. My father died as I approached my ninth birthday.

One morning as I was shooting baskets in the local outdoor court in River Edge, New Jersey, I had a deep sense of God speaking to me. I did not hear an audible voice, but rather I had an intuitive perception of Him speaking to me. The message was, "You should be relating to me." How do I relate to God, I wondered. Then a thought came to me: I should go to a church or a synagogue.

I had cousins whom I liked very much on my mother's side. They always went to Sunday school and church. One Sunday I decided to join them. The church was a lively Evangelical Reformed Church of America congregation. It was there that I heard the Gospel for the first time and decided to make a commitment to the Lord as a result of the inspiring sermon by the guest speaker, George Sweeting.

Soon afterward I decided to go to the Word of Life Camp. There, at the age of 12, I dedicated my life to the Lord. Indeed, I became very committed and very involved during my high school years; Sunday school and church services on Sunday mornings, youth groups and evening services on Sunday nights, and a high school Bible club Monday nights. I spent six summers at Word of Life Camp, first as a camper, then as a counselor in training and finally as a counselor.

Gradually a desire grew in me to know the Lord well, to walk in close fellowship with Him, and eventually, to become a pastor. How my heart burned during great preaching! In high school I was known as "the Preacher." With God's help I went from an obese 278 pounds to a rail at 162 pounds. Those were good years, full of purpose and joy. There were times of backsliding, but in general I lived as a Christian. I loved the church; I would cry during the singing of great hymns and recite the Apostle's Creed* with joy and confidence.

It was during these years that I first became acquainted wth Charismatics. One was Larry Carroll, a saintly elder in the Reformed Church, the other was Judy, the new female youth director. They introduced me to the writings of Andrew Murray and Watchman Nee, and spoke of the deeper spiritual life available through the Baptism in the Spirit. I longed for this experience, and finally I asked them to come lay their hands on me. There was a sense that I had received the Baptism, a release, and we praised God. Although they both spoke in tongues, I did not have the experience at

---

*Ancient Christian statement of faith.

that time. However, they assured me that I had "the Baptism" by faith, even if I didn't speak in tongues.

Great joy followed for many weeks. Bible studies for young people at the home of Larry Carroll were filled with great spiritual fervor and depth. However, I still loved anti-charismatic Word of Life Camp and never separated from other Christians on the basis of this experience. Some left our church because it was not "Spirit-filled," but I loved our church.

Two other experiences influenced me and are worth noting. One was a visit to Teen Challenge in New York City after reading **The Cross and the Switchblade**, by David Wilkerson. Although they clapped and sang with fervor, there was no special manifestation. The other event was a visit to the Manhattan Bible study held in the home of John Macandlish Phillips, the award-winning **New York Times** writer. The "Yale God Squad" (a group of Yale students who were known for bold witnessing) attended these meetings. The study was interesting, and the atmosphere was warm. There was prophecy of a limited nature, but I did not know what to make of it.

After graduation from high school in 1965, I decided to attend the King's College in Westchester County, New York. This was to prepare for an eventual seminary education. King's is a soundly Evangelical college. I thoroughly enjoyed my freshman year, went to summer school and looked forward to my sophomore year. As a sophomore, I found a new girlfriend. Also, I was involved in many extra-curricular activities, including ministerial club, foreign missions club, prayer meetings, and the King's Club visitation team which visited homes for the elderly. Included as well was a heavy academic schedule. I bragged that I only needed four hours of sleep a night, that the Lord was my strength. Then the bottom fell out!

I had thought that my girlfriend was to become my wife, that God had shown by many circumstances that she was "the one!" In getting to know her better, I discovered a deep melancholy which had been hidden underneath an external projection of happiness. Since I was only 19 years old, I found her depressions frightening.

At the same time that I was going through this emotional turmoil, I was also studying the history of philosophy. A question loomed in my mind. Why should I consider Christianity to be true when there are scores of competing world views in the history of philosophy? Why Christianity rather than Hegel, Shopenhauer, or Spinoza? Why not Hinduism? The questions were suppressed until one morning I awoke with the feeling of dread.

I was exhausted and full of guilt and skepticism concerning the truth of Christianity. I was afraid to live and afraid to die. My good friend and roommate Roy Sutten, who had experienced his own trauma, was aware of my state. He knew I was living on a treadmill leading to a crash, but I refused to listen to his advice. After accepting only his empathy, I drove home for Thanksgiving break.

I was in a terrible state. My mother was so alarmed that she took me to our family physician who prescribed rest and gave me antidepressants.

The rest of that year was characterized by fear, depression and skepticism. I commuted to college from home and took fewer courses. Dr. Daniels, a Christian psychiatrist, was a good friend and confidant during those troubled times. He radiated love and patience in his counseling. However, few others seemed to understand my depression. It was not until years later that a firm faith was reestablished.

Because I saw myself becoming too dependent by living at home, and because I wanted to study apologetics, philosophy and world religions on the highest academic level possible, I decided to transfer to Wheaton College in Illinois. After all, I reasoned, if most of King's best professors were "Wheaton grads," why not go to Wheaton? My application was accepted and despite my fears of leaving home, I made the final decision to go.

It was hard to bid farewell to my best friends Ed Demarest, Roy Sutten, and especially to Mom. Leaving the psychiatrist was frightening, too. However, I was convinced I had to take that step to keep myself from becoming a dependent vegetable.

Mom and I drove to Wheaton, and I settled into the new men's dorm. The next day, after driving Mom to the airport, the dread and fear returned. I felt lonely and abandoned and desperately needed some evidence that there was a purpose to the world and a meaning to life.

Someone recommended going to see Chaplain Welsh. He was a saintly man in his sixties, full of love and warmth. His counsel, his love, and the openness of his home became to me a sustaining source of life. He was the most important influence in my return to faith, even though that return was still some years away.

I plunged into classes and the usual collegiate activities. I also heard about a group on campus that gathered for "charismatic worship." They claimed some real miracles. Perhaps this would reveal new evidence of the reality of God. Some of the students in this group were also beginning to attend a church in which the pastor had just received the "Baptism of the Spirit." This was a mainline denominational church attended by many prominent members of a suburban community some 25 minutes from Wheaton. I decided to investigate.

Several events convinced me to attend this church. One was a tape played in Sociology of Religion class. It presented the reality of the Holy Spirit; the teacher on the tape was Kevin Ranigan, the well-known Catholic Charismatic theologian. I learned that my sociology teacher believed the messages of the tape and was going to be attending the Sheepfold Church.

The second event was a chapel talk on the Holy Spirit. Two Wheaton professors presented their views along with the pastor of Sheepfold Church. He testified power-fully of the reality of the gifts of the Holy Spirit and of the manifestations of bona fide supernatural gifts in his church. It was very impressive.

The following weekend two nursing students from Wheaton's West Suburban Nursing School arranged to go on a date with me and Jerry, another Wheaton student whom I had not met before. After we dropped the girls off, Jerry and I remained together discussing many topics. I mentioned my faith struggles and my interest in attending

Sheepfold Church. Jerry excitedly replied that he had recently received the "Baptism in the Holy Spirit," and that he also wanted to go to Sheepfold Church. We made arrangements to go together.

Sunday morning was a momentous day at Sheepfold Church. The service was relatively similar to most mainline churches. However, when the time came to baptize infants, the pastor announced that he could not in good conscience carry out this part of the service. He then gave a sermon in which he explained his new convictions concerning "believer's baptism," tying it to the new move of the Holy Spirit in the congregation. From then on, Sunday morning would never be the same. The gifts of the Spirit would be allowed to flow and only adult believers' baptism by immersion would be practiced. For many old-time members, this marked their last service at Sheepfold Church.

No manifestations of a supernatural character took place at this service. Even so, I was impressed by the courage of Pastor Tabor, especially after I later learned that his stand had cost him about half of his congregation. Previous to his Holy Spirit experience he had been a typical social-activist, mainline-type pastor. After his experience with a local charismatic Episcopal priest, he was ready to turn his church upside down.

Pastor Tabor was a strange man. A combination of shyness and bluntness paradoxically characterized both his public and personal conversation. It was disarming, to say the least. Though I never quite gained an intimate personal understanding of him, a general understanding did develop. I decided I would return to Sheepfold for the Sunday evening service and see if there was a real evidence of the supernatural for apologetic purposes.

This was the age of rebellion; Vietnam was the topic of daily concern. Even at Wheaton, protests and debates were prominent. The old value system seemed to be destined for a major overhaul, or at least a revision. Even Wheaton College could not escape the effects of the sixties. In this context, I found myself sitting in this small circle listening to the prophecies, prayers, scriptures, and Pastor Tabor's rambling messages. Pastor Tabor always gave rambling messages, but they were filled with words of faith and the power of God.

I attended both this church and the campus charismatic prayer group. The worship at Sheepfold was unlike anything I had ever experienced before. There was an outpouring of fervent devotion, a joy, a release in the Spirit, and a spontaneity; yet I was in many ways a bystander, a neutral observer. I had not yet found my "objective" proof of the reality of it all. Perhaps it was only "group-think," in Orwell's terms; perhaps it was only a reflection of the emotionalism of "true believers." Most of the miracles seemed quite minor and amenable to other explanations. Headaches, colds and nebulous pains were cured, but not heart disease, cancer, and atrophied limbs. Yet I continued to attend, hoping perhaps to see the angel of Bethesda stir the waters and produce a bona fide miracle, inexplicable by known natural causes. I even sometimes thought I sensed a presence of God in these services, though I would later discount it. What an amazing thing it was to sing,

> "Let all that is within me cry holy, holy is the lamb that was slain" and "Thou art worthy to receive glory, honor and power. . ."

So I continued to attend the church and to study philosophy, hoping for evidence from some sphere. Chaplain Welsh provided comfort, while my professors provided direction for study. The three most influential were brilliant philosophy teachers, David Wolfe, now of Gordon College, Stuart Hackett of Trinity Divinity School, and Arthur Holmes of Wheaton College.

Then the church underwent **significant** change. First of all, the professor who led the campus charismatic group urged his group to attend Sheepfold. This brought a noticeable addition of students. These students in turn invited others. Though students from other colleges also came, Wheaton predominated.

Secondly, committed older members invited friends and relatives. Many were saved.

Thirdly, several key professors joined: a sociologist, a philosopher, and a communications teacher, all from Wheaton. Indeed, the church was growing. Within a few months all previous membership losses were recovered. The worship was better than ever. Guest preachers such as Ern Baxter provided magnificent preaching and Pastor Tabor continued his rambling sermons.

Sheepfold Church was part of the early charismatic renewal outside of Pentecostalism. Although I could not yet prove the supernatural from personal experience, I was attracted by the vibrant, joyous and reverent worship. During this period, members were encouraged to absorb the teachings of James Beall of Detroit, Derek Prince, Ern Baxter and Harry Greenwood.

The Christmas holiday approached. The church was packed, the worship glorious, and even the message was better than usual. I decided to speak to the pastor after the service concerning my spiritual battles. Perhaps he could add some new light.

Jerry came with me into the pastor's study. I explained my problem and Pastor Tabor replied, "Your problem is that you need the Baptism in the Holy Spirit." Well, perhaps so, I thought. Maybe it would be so directly supernatural that my doubts would be gone. Therefore I submitted to the laying on of hands. As they prayed in tongues and urged me to join in, I found myself speaking forth a torrent of new unlearned syllables. Indeed, we prayed and sang in tongues for quite a while. Jerry was ecstatic. He even prayed that the nature of the tongue might change and professed that as he prayed, my syllables changed to a different type of language.

What was this experience? Was it a real language? Was it proof of God? The questions raced through my mind, but I felt it better not to discuss them with my ecstatic friend Jerry. All during the Christmas break I continued to speak in tongues while still raising the same questions. Indeed, I later found many books and articles explaining what was called "glossolalia" from many different perspectives. Some explained it psychologically, others anthropologically; some claimed it was a real language, others

said it was nonsense. Still others held it to
be a linguistic expression with some of the
characteristics of a real language but without others. What confusion!

However, I returned to my studies at
Wheaton to seek rational-empirical evidence for meaning and purpose while still
attending Sheepfold Church to look for a
true miracle. This was a very significant
period for me because I was intensely
studying Eastern religious philosophy. My
critical abilities began to gel as I read
theology, philosophy, and church history
with greater ease and understanding. The
ability to compare and contrast viewpoints
was crucial in evaluating the next eighteen
months.

At Wheaton, I met a new friend in the
oratorio choir just before Christmas break.
His name was Jack Colpepper. Jack was of
Mennonite extraction and the son of a
deceased Baptist minister. He was a very
lovable person with a warm ear-to-ear
smile. One day I mentioned to him that I
was looking for a new roommate. "So am I,"
he blurted out. We therefore decided to room
together.

Also during this time, the charismatic
philosophy professor who attended Sheepfold and I were developing a relationship.
He encouraged me to take a more existen-
tial approach to events and to recognize

that knowledge is derived from faith. Dr. Ziegler was a warm and accepting person, but I had difficulty with his "faith-approach" to these significant questions. I identified with the hard-nosed rational approach of Dr. Hackett, professor of Philosophy of Religion.

One day, soon after Jack and I became roommates, I invited Jack to accompany me to Sheepfold Church. "Perhaps you could give me your opinion; it might be helpful," I added.

When the service was over, I asked for his opinion. He said, "This is the New Testament church!" Jack proceeded to become an ardent member of the church; other friends followed. I desired to participate fully, but could not seem to lose my objective distance from it all.

Our group of friends consisted of Bill, a brilliant young man who was training to be a European missionary, his girlfriend Janice, and Jerry's new girlfriend Mary. We were a unique group. Sometimes my friends bore with me; other times they chastised me; and at worst they avoided me. However, they were my college friends.

So the year continued. Studies progressed. The true miracle did not occur. Summer vacation came.

The following fall I picked up where I had left off. This was a year of great transition in the church. There were new phenomena such as directive prophecy and various thrusts in evangelism. The greatest significance, however, was a slow but steady progress in the church toward a new and bizarre understanding of the Bible and of the proper approach to it.

There was a good service one particular October evening. I remember it well. Pastor Tabor gave an unusually coherent message, and afterward I complimented him on it. "Did you receive it with your intellect or with your spirit?" he replied.

I answered, "With both."

This incident is an illustration of a gradual turn to new attitudes and perspectives. A great emphasis was placed on the pride of the intellect. The intellect was considered a barrier to true spiritual understanding. The pastor and many of the students spoke of Evangelicalism as a dead intellectual faith. A sharp demarcation was made between "Spirit-filled" Christians and "non-Spirit-filled." This seemed ludicrous to me, since some very immature people described themselves as "Spirit-filled," while they would say of Chaplain Welsh, for example, that he was not Spirit-filled.

I questioned, "How can a saintly, loving and kind person who gives testimony of many spiritual experiences of a supernatural kind not be Spirit-filled," while these immature folks who speak in tongues are "Spirit-filled"? Can we really make "speaking in tongues" and "Spirit-filled" synonymous terms?

When I raised these questions with my circle of friends, I was told that the problem was my intellect. I now realize that there **is** a pride of the intellect that is a great barrier to receiving spiritual truth. Yet, do we not need to weigh the issues of evidence and truth in the mind? I wrestled with a slow but definite development of an anti-intellectual tone that began to grow at Sheepfold Church.

The preaching that fall began to emphasize Romans 6. This passage, on our co-death and resurrection with Jesus, was tied very closely to a new emphasis on baptism. There was a great emphasis on the need for all to be fully immersed in the **name of Jesus** for the specific cutting off of the old person. It was emphasized that baptism was a **real work**, a necessity to complete the salvation experience. Prophetic words confirmed this message.

That fall I met my future wife. She was related to another Sheepfold member in our circle of friendship. We would all discuss the teaching and prophecy coming forth at the church. Soon, most of us were convinced of the need to be rebaptized. Some, like myself, had never been immersed. Scripturally, it was something I sensed I should do to ensure that I had fully obeyed all of Scripture. My girlfriend Patty, several friends, and I were rebaptized by Pastor Tabor. In our case, I thought, perhaps we would be given greater faith-ability through this action.

It was a glorious service at the rented facilities of the local Baptist church. The singing was exuberant, the testimonies exciting, and the response of applause and joy for each baptized person was a shout of victory. How well I remember the people that night! There was my roommate Jack, his great smile beaming; the quiet joyous look of the sociology professor. There were Jerry and Mary. They looked at me with an expression which said, "Now you will finally be truly one with us."

Mary had originally fled in terror from the manifestations of the campus prayer meeting. Now, however, she was convinced by both Jerry and her own searching that this was right.

Also present were Bill, our suite-mate, and his girlfriend Janice, an exuberant, tall and plump girl from a Pentecostal background. Bill kept telling me I had a skeptical mindset, not real intellectual problems with the faith. Janice spoke of her personal experience with the power of God.

How I loved them all; such good people. Yet how the doubts still lingered!

Patty and I continued to share our burdens with Chaplain Welsh. He gave warmth, spoke well of those who claimed he was not "Spirit-filled," and gave us hope and affirmation.

It was a busy fall. I had become the assistant in Philosophy of Religion to Dr. Stuart Hackett, a brilliant lecturer with a classical Thomistic perspective. The dichotomy was a real tension. The church was tainted with anti-intellectualism, but my course of study and my responsibilities were highly intellectual. However, the anti-intellectualism was not yet that severe. In fact, the intellectual members interpreted the anti-intellectual bias to be more an expression against false rationalistic approaches in thinking and not opposed to the proper use of the intellect. Therefore, I hoped that greater balance and clarity would come and the tension would be lessened.

Later that fall, several of the Sheepfold students of Wheaton had prophetic words of a directive nature within their prayer groups. One led to my roommate Jack going with an attractive, bright-eyed enthusiastic girl named Susan. Another confirmed the marriage of Jerry and Mary.

Jerry was a Junior and Mary was a

Sophomore. Mary's parents were against the marriage, but they acquiesced when Mary held firm. Mary's folks were unhappy at the service and her dad was short and critical with Jerry. Yet the wedding went forward. Jack, Bill, Mary, Patty and I were all in the wedding party. Everyone in the college Sheepfold circle confirmed this marriage despite the parents' objections.

It didn't go well with Jack and Susan, however. He found himself in conflict with her; they were not "flowing" together. They tried to feel love, but it was not forthcoming. Finally Jack decided to speak to a charismatic leader at a conference in Detroit. After much discussion with Susan, he decided to break the relationship. As a result of some of these experiences it was decided to no longer have prayer groups operating separately from church authority.

Life continued as always until the night of the "great miracle." We gathered for an especially powerful evening of worship. In the past when I would question the Sheepfold Church, Jack would often say, "You know it is of God; where else is there an expression of worship to compare with it?" That evening was certainly a demonstration of Jack's words.

During the period of prophecy, a mother brought her child for healing. Apparently, her legs were paralyzed. A group gathered in a circle to lay hands on her and pray. Finally they took the girl by the hand and began to encourage her to walk. She took a feeble step with adult support. People began to praise God in song. She took another step. They praised more loudly. She took two shaky slow steps by herself, and they began to praise with all their might. The little girl walked, and finally ran to her mother. Everyone was ecstatic. Joy and exaltation were thicker than can be imagined. A new day had dawned.

This was the opportunity I had longed for: a possible **bona fide** miracle. I had to find the mother after the service and obtain the medical records.

It took awhile to break through the throng of people congratulating her. When I did, I asked a question no one had thought to ask. "What was wrong with your child?"

Her answer was, "Oh, nothing I can pin down. She came home from school yesterday and plopped on the floor saying, 'Mommy, I cannot walk.' I took her to the doctor and he said there was nothing wrong with her, that she was just going through a psychological stage and when she wants to walk she will."

What a let down! I too was praising and believing at last that this might be a biblical-type miracle. Now it seemed clear:

It was only the crowd encouragement which gave the girl the motivation to walk.

With my friends, traveling home, I shared my disappointment. They discounted it by saying, "A healing is a healing." If it was only psychological, it was a wonderful healing of the girl's emotions. They missed the point of my concern. An emotional healing carried no apologetic evidential value.

Over the next week on campus, I was surprised to hear the spread of the story of a great supernatural miracle. It was said that an amazing healing of a paralytic had taken place and had been witnessed by hundreds. Invitations to attend Sheepfold Church were given to students. These invitations included the story of healing.

I was upset by this turn of events. I saw it as deceptive. Therefore, I went to talk with Dr. Ziegler, the Christian Existentialist philosopher. He encouraged me not to get "bent out of shape", that psychological healing was important, that no one was intentionally deceiving, and that I should just let it pass. Perhaps if we would receive the power of God by faith for small things (colds, aches, and psychological problems) we would later see healing in the areas of tumors and atrophied limbs.

"Be patient and seek to develop faith," he counseled.

Seeking to pin down a miracle was very difficult. I would hear of a cancerous tumor which was healed, but when I would check it out it proved far from certain. Once Jerry claimed he saw a cancer tumor disappear. I questioned how he knew it was cancer. He replied that he assumed the lump on the man's neck was cancer.

"Did it really disappear?" I asked.

"Well, sort of," he replied, "although it didn't go away completely, it appeared to me to shrink."

I was having a very hard time finding a real miracle at Sheepfold Church, and I wondered how many miracles in the charismatic movement were the product of the same wishful thinking and enthusiasm I had seen at Sheepfold.

Since that time, I am thrilled to say, I have more than substantiated many **bona fide** miracles. Most of them have been in charismatic circles, though many were also in noncharismatic groups. The first was a Lutheran friend who was healed at the point of death from a severed main artery in his neck. He is today a minister. Many of Kathryn Kuhlman's miracles are authentic and one of her case histories described a student at Wheaton. This wasn't enough to settle all my faith questions, however. There seemed to be real miracles, though not at Sheepfold Church.

During the winter several tendencies became an established and pronounced part of Sheepfold's **perspective**. This new viewpoint was one of the main factors responsible for our leaving Sheepfold.

Several members of the congregation had been convinced that practical perfection was possible on the basis of the baptism in the Holy Spirit. From this practical perfection would come an amazing number of miraculous manifestations. When sin was still manifested in their lives, they were greatly discouraged. Anger, lust, selfishness, impure thoughts and anxiety were still experienced from time to time. Perfectionism proved to be a doctrine of discouragement.

Furthermore, many began to see that the miracle stories that had been so enthusiastically spread were very insubstantial. It seemed as if the sense of the miraculous grew more and more dim. This was the age in which theologians were saying "God is dead," or at least is hidden. To many at Sheepfold, it seemed as if God were indeed hidden. Unfulfilled expectations led to discouragement which confirmed this fear. Why would this be? Hadn't we received the Holy Spirit baptism? Did we not go through water baptism in the name of Jesus with faith in the cutting off of the old person?

The response of the pastor was expressed through his teaching. First, it was emphasized that our private interpretations of Scripture needed to be submitted to the body. Indeed, the body was said to be the source for our understanding of Scripture. Apart from the church, it was said, we really could not adequately understand the Scriptures.

At first this emphasis was very low key. Many understood it to mean that we needed the input of brothers and sisters and leadership to come to fuller understanding in the Spirit. Whenever the question of the authority of the Bible came up, Pastor Tabor would assure everyone that his speech wasn't yet clear in expressing the revelation of the importance of the church as a teaching authority.

"Don't worry about it at this time, since it is not yet clear."

Yet over the next year this emphasis grew to the point at which some gave up reading the Bible altogether so as to get their teaching only from the church.

The church, under the leadership of Pastor Tabor's teaching, and prophetic messages that would come from the members, developed several significant doctrines. **First**, it was said that the church needed to go through a wilderness period before entering the promised land of miracles and perfection. This was the process of dying with Christ (Romans 6). The preaching, week after week, emphasized only Romans 6 and the Israel wilderness experience. Dying with Christ and going through the wilderness could take a long time. We were not yet dead and resurrected.

The **second** development was a subtle but steady growth in the doctrine which stated that the intellect was a primary barrier to receive spiritual things. The "crucifixion of the intellect" doctrine became more prominent toward the end of 1969.

Shortly before I left the church, the editor of the campus magazine and I had a conversation. She had heard that I planned to attend Trinity Evangelical Divinity School for a Philosophy of Religion degree. She asked, "Isn't that against your faith?"

"I hope not," I said.

Indeed, if the mind does not weigh truth and test for error, how shall we avoid falling into falsehood? We must "test the spirits."

This anti-intellect doctrine slowly evolved into a reaction against what was called "dead Evangelical orthodoxy," which was said to be a gangrene to spiritual life, a destructive cancer. Some students influenced by a neo-orthodox view of Scripture applauded these teachings. They held that the Scripture is not the Word, but only becomes the Word when used by the Spirit in the context of the church. This is the essence of the neo-orthodox view. Due to the prominence of this view, I found myself attending less often.

The **last doctrine** held that we were **awaiting the formation of Christ in us**. We were in the pangs of birth waiting to deliver. I John's references to Jesus' coming in the flesh were interpreted to mean Jesus being formed in the body. Several questioned this view and noted that these passages referred to the heresies that claimed Jesus really didn't become human flesh. The historic context of I John is a reply to those who denied the **real incarnation** (into flesh) of the Lord. The response by Pastor Tabor was that the intellect was blocking spiritual truth, that we needed to receive spiritual truth spiritually.

He also denied that in teaching this spiritual application he was saying any-thing contrary to the historic incarnation. But what was considered important was the **spiritual meaning** of the passage as **the Spirit** was **applying it in our present situa-tion**. The overconcern with historic events was said to be a false pre-occupation of dead orthodoxy.

Of crucial significance was Sheepfold's relationship to the rest of the church during these times. The doctrines taught by Pastor Tabor were strongly affirmed by the prophetic flow during the service, and by the members outside of the service—by amazing dreams, visions and prophecies. Yet other church leaders questioned the direction Pastor Tabor was taking, especially in regard to the I John interpretations and the "manifest sons of God" doctrine.

This latter doctrine emphasized the second coming or return of Jesus as having reference to his coming in the church, or the church being perfected in Him. At Sheepfold, both the **incarnation** (his coming in the flesh) and the second coming were being spoken of more and more in terms of Jesus being formed in us: the congregational body being brought to perfection or the resurrection life of Jesus in us. However, it was constantly emphasized that we were in the crucifixion stage, the wilderness stage, or the dying stage. Other leaders who had related to Sheepfold (Ern Baxter, Rev. James Beall) began to get wind of this doctrine. They sought to impress upon Pastor Tabor that Sheepfold's teaching was in error, especially in regard to the interpretation of Jesus coming in the flesh.

Pastor Tabor's response was withdrawal. He proceeded to subtly tell the congregation that the church was being misunderstood. With great delicacy he shared that Sheepfold Church was **hearing from God in a unique way** that only could be truly understood by the involved members. For a time, until God revealed the same doctrine to others, Sheepfold would need to go through a period of separation, or at least distance from other leaders and congregations. By this separation, God would be able to do his unique work without the confusion and hindrance that would come from other leadership input.

Sheepfold now had established a **pattern of inwardness** and church authority which dominated the lives of its members. For many, their only understanding of Scripture came from the church and there was no input from other leaders. Patty (my future wife) and I could not tolerate any longer the subjectivity of Sheepfold. If our mind did not test doctrine by an objective reading of Scripture, anything could be possible. Hence, after June 1969, we left Sheepfold for good, though we maintained close contact with **several** Sheepfold members for the next **few** years.

It might be asked how students from Evangelical homes could be so easily drawn into the new doctrines of Sheepfold. It should be understood that the process of indoctrination was gradual and subtle. Pastor Tabor would speak of some aspects of a new doctrine. Usually a significant minority reacted negatively. The Pastor's response to this negative feedback was to pull away saying, "I didn't mean it that way," or "The Spirit is not yet clear enough and we mustn't prejudge until there is greater clarity," or "Let's put this on the back burner because I'm not yet sure if I spoke correctly." This would satisfy the critics.

Amazingly, however, prophetic words and vivid dreams would confirm the message over the weeks to follow. Later the pastor would again teach the doctrine with new aspects. This time fewer would object. People began to see how it could be so; they got used to the idea. Again there would be a partial pullback. After several times of putting forth a teaching and pulling back, after many months of prophetic confirmation, eventually almost everyone accepted the doctrine. Those who could not left the church.

Because of the closeness of the community which developed, there was a great social pressure to see it the pastor's way. Pastor Tabor was not a strong, domineering leader; yet the pressure was great. If a person did not accept the doctrine, he would lose his friends, the affirming sense of closeness in community, indeed, the whole social support system which developed. Because doctrine slowly evolved with a pulsation of putting forth and withdrawing, people became desensitized to the most radical points of view. They got used to the ideas. It was like the proverbial frog: dropped in boiling water, he would jump out immediately. Yet put into a pot which was slowly brought to a boil, the frog would become accustomed to the gradual increase in temperature and would do nothing.

Another important dimension was the view of and attitude toward Evangelicalism and Fundamentalism. Both were characterized as dead, legalistic and intellectualistic at best, and a cancer or gangrene at worst. Some students, who were bitter over legalistic backgrounds and quite negative toward Wheaton, their parents and their home church, became influential in the direction of the congregation through the prophetic flow. They would share their prophetic sense with Pastor Tabor, who referred to it as confirmation of his teaching. Pastor Tabor was influenced in his view of Wheaton and Evangelicalism by the views that came from the students. Dreams were also given prominent exposure through mutual sharing privately or in the services. Prophecy also confirmed previously formed views of Evangelicals. Evangelical circles which were anti-charismatic were pointed to so as to confirm the judgment.

How did this affect people personally? My roommate, Jack, began to doubt the value of his studies. However, there was still a mixture of opinion, even in his own mind. At times he still hoped for a reconciliation between the values of education at Wheaton and the spiritual-prophetic dimensions of Sheepfold. Perhaps Sheepfold was really only speaking of an overly intellectualistic approach; perhaps there was a balanced spiritual approach to study. However, at other times the whole Christian liberal arts endeavor was questioned.

It was a time of turmoil for Jack, but he could not leave Sheepfold because the spiritual experience was so dramatically real for him. His experience was paralleled by many others, some of whom came from the ranks of the brighter students at Wheaton. Part of the attraction to Sheepfold was a new spiritual security in which one had a rationale for not having to deal with the hard questions and challenges to faith brought by the study of philosophy, psychology and literature. If these subjects made us uncomfortable and challenged an easy faith, Sheepfolders felt perhaps they were suspect. Some who were in the midst of faith reevaluation due to exposure through their studies were feeling adrift indeed. The **innovative** perspective of Sheepfold gave them a **new** sense of the reality of the supernatural.

Some began to **bifurcate** valid and invalid studies. Many became sociology majors; it was practical. Others saw the natural sciences as valid. Philosophy, theology, literature, anthropology and psychology became forbidden territory. Of course, this **dichotomy** is totally invalid since all sciences raise significant philosophical issues. Conflicting philosophies of science certainly prove this.

One student who left Sheepfold finally rejected the whole Sheepfold mentality. He said to his friend Jeff, "Why don't you refuse your diploma if you really believe in crucifying the intellect?" Jeff accepted the diploma for its pragmatic value in the job market, but otherwise said he would be glad to burn it.

Other students dropped out of school and went to work. For a time this was the case with Jerry and Mary. Eventually Jerry enrolled in another school for a sociology degree for practical purposes. Bill and his girlfriend Janice took a different approach. It was to slide by and get the degree but do as little work as possible. He sought to get C's and eventually to get the degree for practical job purposes. This brilliant philosophy student who was burdened to become a missionary to France now no longer desired either to go to France or to finish his studies. Eventually he married our friend Janice. This approach led to his flunking out of school the following year. These patterns were often **repeated** by others.

The 1969 to 1970 period brought little significant change. The doctrines of Sheepfold Church became more and more solidified. We were amazed to learn that Sheepfold was still going through the wilderness and waiting for the resurrection.

Other significant events and directions should be reported. I was a weekly visitor to Wheaton in the 1969-1970 school year because Patty was still a student there. I would stay in one of the men's houses which included several Sheepfold members. I noticed that many were identifying emotionally with aspects of the "hip" culture, the new-left, and the whole "rock scene." Bill began to do pop art. It reflected a deep cynicism for modern American life. Others began to identify with the last, most pessimistic messages of the Beatles. The only real hope in their view was Sheepfold.

A conversation with Jack that fall was most alarming, but it paralleled the convictions of many Sheepfold members. When I argued with Jack over Scriptural teaching and issues the argument usually came to a disagreement of method between Jack's subjective approach to Scripture and my objective approach. Finally Jack said, "Dan, I don't believe that we can understand the

Bible unless it comes through the teaching of the church. Only the teaching of the church is important to me."

My response was, "Jack, I believe that the church is very important. However, the Scripture must be the source for evaluating the church. Sometimes a church goes into error and it becomes our responsibility to leave the church. When Martin Luther started the Reformation, he was summoned to appear before the Emperor to defend himself. His interrogator asked him, "Martin, how is it that you presume to stand against the judgment of Popes and councils and even the whole tradition of church interpretation?" Luther replied, "Whether there be Popes, they have erred and sinned, councils have gone astray. If anyone can convince me from the Scriptures that I am in error, I shall wholly repent. However, if not, I must say that my mind is captive to the Word of God. Here I stand, I can do no other."

"What if Sheepfold Church goes into gross error? What will you do? Will you not have to choose God and the Word over and above a particular church?"

Jack answered, "I cannot separate my commitment to God from my commitment to Sheepfold. They are one and the same. If Sheepfold goes down the tubes, I go with it."

At this point I realized that the battle was lost. There was no further argument. Sheepfold's members had given up the ability of independent evaluation.

Similar conversations were held with Jerry and Mary with the same frustrating results. There was no way to break through. There was no point of common ground from which to argue them out of their previously drawn conclusions.

My first year at Trinity was still a period of doubt and searching. However, little by little God began to reveal himself to me and studies began to confirm the Scriptures. By the end of 1970, God had supernaturally spoken to my heart via the Word, dreams and study. I now was clearly becoming established in the faith. At Trinity I saw great piety merged with scholarship in such wonderful men as Dr. R. Longenecker, Dr. K. Kantzer, Dr. E. Harrison and Dr. David Wells. It was a marvelously liberating experience. Patty and I found ourselves growing more and more apart from Sheepfold friends, some of whom had been our closest friends. We attended an Evangelical Lutheran church under a dear, saintly pastor, Rev. Theodore Laesch. His example and teaching provided a healing experience. The Lutheran service of communion was a beautiful means to draw us close to God. We even considered the Lutheran pastorate. Continued contact with Dr. Welsh was still greatly restorative.

During this period, Dr. Welsh also became alarmed at the trends of Sheepfold. He who had been so open and accepting was now definitely opposed. The year 1971 saw Sheepfold members adopt the posture of refusing to visit other churches. "They are dead places of idolatry," they said.

Parents and children became severely divided. Indeed, it was the Sheepfold perspective that it might be necessary for some to cut off relationships with parents.

At this time we also began to perceive a strange looseness among some Sheepfold members. Speech included swear words and other loose, demeaning language.

At Trinity I met a new friend, Russ Savage. Russ, a tall, lanky Canadian, was a philosophical thinker in the same Trinity program as I. He, Patty and I were invited to a party at Jerry and Mary's apartment. The lights were dim, the rock music blared, and the Sheepfold members at the party danced with sensual abandon. Some retired to other rooms to share passionate embracing and kissing. We saw no nudity nor any blatant sinful activities. Yet the atmosphere was sensually charged.

After the party, Russ remarked, "Listen, that group is weird. I've been involved with secular groups at the University; I've been to their parties. I've even seen them degenerate into sin. But that was just plain old-fashioned secular sin. This party had a strange dimension. It was something on another level. These people were expressing deep negative reactions to their background as part of their sin. There was an attitude and atmosphere that is thoroughly unhealthy beyond anything I've experienced."

I agreed with Russ. How perceptive were his words! The previous summer I had spoken with the elder, Larry Carroll, who had first introduced me to the "baptism in the Spirit." When I explained the treatment of Scripture at Sheepfold, he predicted, "The next step is immorality." Indeed, the next few years at Sheepfold were momentous as elements of destruction came to full manifestation.

Contacts with Sheepfold members during the next two years were less frequent. However, there was enough contact to produce a significant amount of insight. As the year 1971 progressed, Sheepfold members became more intensely permeated by the concept of the wilderness state of their existence. They accepted themselves as spiritually dead and in need of resurrection. Their hope was in a supernatural renewal that would produce immediate perfection. The only spiritual reality was the prophetic dimension at Sheepfold. The members were more and more withdrawn into their own community.

The leadership at Sheepfold emphasized the importance of not visiting other communities, and no longer sharing the revelation coming forth with people outside the community. "They wouldn't understand."

Patty and I were exceptions to this rule. First, we were perceived as more open and still searching. Second, we had been close friends with the members. The changes during 1971 were not totally radical. Members became more tightly knit. They partied together, worked together and waited together.

Bill and Janice lived in a small bungalow and drifted into a more and more nihilistic concept of life while maintaining their Sheepfold hope. He began to develop an interest in auto mechanics which would eventually provide his living. Jack worked at various jobs not requiring specific training. He gained an interest in large motorcycles and wore granny glasses. This was an incredible change in Jack's personality.

Jerry began to develop an interest in computers. It was a financially good field. This became his eventual career choice. The sociology professor continued to teach her classes; they became more and more contentless. The philosophy teacher, Dr. Ziegler transferred to a secular college but no longer sought to find truth in philosophy.

Many people experienced great conflicts in their marriages. In addition, many found it necessary to cut off relationships with old friends and relatives, especially parents. Parents became alarmed, but found no way to correct the errors they saw or to regain the trust of their children. Slowly the character of our friends also began to change.

There was more and more willingness to use loose language and to indulge in worldly entertainment. Not only seedy rock music, but R and X-rated motion pictures were considered acceptable. "It is good to know the real world," some would say.

It was considered important to break out of fundamentalist strictures. The goals of many became more focused upon immediate pleasures. For some, this was reflected in materialistic desires, for others in the adoption of the appearance and attitudes of the sixties counterculture. Covert fornication among singles, and possibly even others, began at this time, but it was not condoned behavior.

Slowly, the atmosphere of the church began to change as well. This evolution followed the theology of the church. "If we are spiritually dead, in the process of dying or going through the wilderness, how can we be singing worship songs and taking the Lord's supper? Does baptism even work in our present situation?"

These questions led to a gradual cessation of these practices. The services became primarily an exercise in hearing revelation and in absorbing the sermons of Pastor Tabor. During this period the church began to lose members. Some saw no point to it at all. Sheepfold had been their last hope; as a result they became secular. Others went back to Evangelical expressions of faith. Still others said they still believed in Sheepfold, but did not really need to attend at this point. The leaders of Sheepfold saw this as a necessary stage toward the goal of perfection.

"We are being pruned and getting to the real core of our membership," Pastor Tabor said. "When the resurrection comes, all those who have been connected to us will return." This was all part of the wilderness experience. The Sheepfold members subjectively spiritualized and allegorized all things.

The following year I accepted my first pastorate in Chicago at the First Hebrew Christian Church. Chaplain Welsh had been interim pastor and recommended me to the elders. Eventually I was ordained in the

United Presbyterian Church.

The limited experiences with Sheepfold members were extremely valuable for obtaining information. Jerry and Mary related much to us and Jack filled in many of the gaps. We learned that various couples were separating, some even were seeking divorce. This included our friends Janice and Bill.

What a tragedy! The future missionary to France, the brilliant student, and his Pentecostal wife; how their lives seemed ruined. We didn't know the half of it. The next few visits with Jerry and Mary provided all the necessary details.

As we sat together, we probed Jerry and Mary for updated information on Sheepfold church. Our friends had become part of the inner core. Finally the bombshell was dropped. Mary had given herself to extra-marital affairs. Jerry had committed adultery as well. However, we were told not to be alarmed because it was all part of the process leading to the resurrection and perfection of the Church. Many of the young couples had swapped mates and had extra-marital affairs. Bill had moved in with a forty-plus woman.

How was this all justified? Mary explained their reasoning. "If we really are in a spiritually dead state or dying process waiting for the resurrection, then to continue to seek to follow a rigid morality would only be hypocrisy. To give in to the desires within us would be a step of honesty. When Pastor Tabor first heard about various members sleeping together, he expressed worry that it could destroy Sheepfold. Yet, he realized it might be a necessary stage in the process toward the resurrection. Indeed, there was revelation to confirm that this was a necessary stage. The physical nature is not all that important; therefore, to indulge it does not matter. What is important is not physical adultery, but spiritual adultery or idolatry. Evangelicals are unresurrected and are making a pretense of morality though they are obviously imperfect. This is spiritual adultery; a terrible sin. Since they are dead, but yet are worshipping in their services, they must be serving and worshipping a false god. We shouldn't be preoccupied with sex, but at this stage, if we must indulge, it is better to do so than to live in the tension which comes from resisting. I have had two dreams to confirm this. When I explained them to Pastor Tabor, he confirmed them. They speak to the situation of the church.

"In one I was sitting on a river bank beneath a dam full of water. The the dam burst. I was full of fear and sought to escape from the rush of the water, but I could not. After the flood I found myself in a place of

calm and peace farther downstream where
the waters no longer raged. I was swept
along but unharmed. The waters repre-
sented stored up passions and desires. They
had to be released. However, releasing them
would not ultimately harm me.

"In the other dream a one-horned beast
charged me and pushed its horn into my
chest. Rather than dying, although it hurt, I
felt purified or cleansed. The bull's horn
was a phallus. When it was plunged in, I
was cleansed."

Mary lay with a secular man who was
not part of Sheepfold. She described it as
enjoyable because he was a "neat guy," but
also painful in a way. Jerry had an experience of a similar kind. Now that they had
done this, they claimed they were freer and
not hung up. They could attend nude bars,
or other worldly places, without being up-
tight. Others were having similar experiences. It was all part of waiting for the
resurrection.

I expressed my disagreement, but I
knew if I opposed them too strongly, they
would have left our company for good.
Mary was amazingly "hung up" about the
mistakes and harm her parents had caused.
This surfaced constantly in conversation.

I reflected during this conversation on
how similar this teaching was to the
heretics in the early centuries of the church

who were called **libertarian gnostics**. They had rigidly divided the spiritual and the physical. The latter was of no consequence. Therefore, the indulgence of the flesh proved its insignificance and liberated the spirit. As Ecclesiastes says, "There is nothing new under the sun."

The last extensive visit we had with Mary and Jerry shed further light on the situation of Sheepfold. The teaching had taken on a decidedly Eastern twist. They were seeking the God beyond God who could not be spoken of but was only to be experienced beyond concepts and words. However, words were said to be vehicles to break down all the illusions of false religion so we could experience the true God. Historical knowledge was unimportant. The resurrection of Jesus was not denied, but the question of its historical reality was unimportant since its only significant meaning was the spiritual resurrection to come.

"It makes no difference whether it happened in the physical," they said. "Jesus' coming in the flesh is his being formed in us."

I was able to probe the question with such understanding that Mary was amazed. This proved to them that I was really part of the fold. However, I explained to them that I was a student of Eastern religious philosophy, and this was why I understood.

In fact, their view was not a new revelation at all. When I told them this, it strained our visit. It was the last really **significant** contact with them, during which we also learned that one of the sources of revelation at Sheepfold was the son of a Buddhist priest who had married one of the Wheaton students!

Later, at a Wheaton football game, we met Janice. We asked her if she still attended Sheepfold. She said she didn't, but she still felt a part of it. She explained that she was living a secular life and enjoying her "freedom."

"I am a healthy, red-blooded female animal, you know."

Then one morning the phone rang.

"Hello, Dan? This is Jack. How are you?"

"Fine, and you?"

"Not too good, I'm in the hospital. Would you like to visit with me?"

Jack was a patient in a renowned psychiatric hospital in the area. He had crashed.

The experience with Jack which followed this phone call gave me many missing details about Sheepfold. Through him I learned much concerning the sources and implications of cultic bondage.

As we sat in Jack's hospital room, he told me some of the sad details that led to his hospitalization. He described a more rampant sexual looseness among couples than we had even imagined. There were parties that ended in orgies. Drugs were also part of the experience among some. He stated that some of the parties even took on a "Charles Manson type atmosphere." "There was such suspicion that I thought it would end in violence."

Drugs, women and conceptual confusion produced an identity crisis in Jack. Some others were even into astrology as a means of understanding reality. This was prevalent among younger rather than older members.

The night Jack "freaked out," he was thinking that he was John the Baptist. He was taken to the hospital, paranoid to the extreme. Pastor Tabor signed him in. When the door locked behind him in the ward, he went berserk and had to be strapped down. He was having delusions and had also experienced some fearful drug flashbacks. Since Pastor Tabor had previously referred to Jack as Sheepfold's John the Baptist, a forerunner of what the church would eventually come to, the direction of Jack's delusion was understandable.

Jack was blessed with a fine psychiatrist, a man open to the spiritual dimensions of psychiatric problems. After therapy and treatment, Jack was eventually able to be released for visits with us and finally came to stay as a boarder.

Seeing Jack "freak out" really disturbed Jerry and Mary. Jerry was on the verge of breaking from Sheepfold. However, even though he was in a state of real anxiety, he was unable to break away. Furthermore, his wife was holding firm.

When Jack came to live with us he was full of fear, bitterness, anxiety, mistrust, irrational thought and doublemindedness. Why had he been allowed to be so deceived? he wondered. At times he slipped back into the Sheepfold mentality. Twice he ran away—once even running back to Sheepfold and another time to New York State where a former Sheepfold member who had a similar experience had found help in a Christian community. For a time he lived with his very worried mother and step-father. Yet he found help and promise in being with us.

His psychiatrist and I could provide greater counsel and understanding. So finally Jack returned to stay with Patty and me. This lasted until his marriage.

After walking off many jobs within the first few days because of waves of un-controllable fear, Jack stuck with a job as a cab driver. With much counsel, conversa-tion and prayer, including the dimensions of deliverance from occult bondage, Jack came to a real state of psychological health. The medication was discontinued. He became his old self. The broad smile and the love of life returned: he was healed.

Why
Did It
Happen?

II. WHY DID IT HAPPEN?

We are entering a phase of history in which social upheaval is prevalent. If at any time in history stable mature leadership was needed in the church, today matches that time. This brings us to our first reason for the tragedies of Sheepfold Church: inadequate leadership. All the factors to be discussed are crucial danger signs. They should awaken reservations before deciding to join or continue with any particular congregation, but the first factor is especially vital.

A. Inadequacy of Leadership According to Biblical Criteria

Pastor Tabor was not the usual image of cultic leader. He was not domineering; he did not command the worship or adoration of his followers. He certainly was stubborn once he had formed a conviction, yet he often seemed a victim of circumstance beyond his own control.

The experience of Sheepfold convinced me that a strong cultic figure is not necessary for the development of a devastatingly destructive cultic community. **Inadequacy of leadership, however, seems always to be a crucial factor.**

Pastor Tabor was a liberal Protestant with **little solid biblical background**. When he and his church switched from the liberal-humanistic mode to evangelical-charismatic, Pastor Tabor had little background or qualification to lead the congregation in its new mode of belief. There was very **limited** background for **spiritual discernment**. In truth, Pastor Tabor was a new believer, and new believers are not quickly to be raised to leadership or they can be puffed up with pride (I Timothy 3:6).

It was pride that led to Pastor Tabor's refusal to hear and be corrected by other leaders. Hence, he cut off relations with the rest of the church. As a new believer, he was ill-prepared to deal with the spiritual phenomena at Sheepfold. Soon liberal ideas concerning Scriptural inspiration and authority from his seminary studies were drawn upon when they fit the need to break from Scripture to support ecstatic prophecies and dreams.

Pastor Tabor's own spiritual stability was of real concern. He often exhibited depression, confusion, mood swings and personal pride and hurt. There was certainly a measure of compassion and some desire for truth, yet pride superseded it. Because Pastor Tabor had never been a **leader under proper spiritual authority**, he did not know how to lead in a proper spiritual manner.

The possibilities of a variety of motives and inspirations in prophecy escaped his perception. The intricacies of human depravity and its manifestations in individuals and groups were certainly not part of his spiritual training or experience.

Other people in leadership at Sheepfold were as weak in experience as Pastor Tabor, with one exception. This was an elder with an evangelical seminary background, but he was swept along with the congregation. Although there were a few professors of the Christian college who went along with the teaching of Sheepfold, they were not in direct leadership. They were either weak in personal stability or had exhibited a history of hurt and disappointment. Some who did not exhibit a psychological instability were **spiritually and theologically weak** even though they were well educated in their respective academic disciplines.

Leadership which is weak in spiritual experience, biblical theology and personal stability is dangerous leadership. I have come to the conclusion that a stable, satisfying family life is a literal prerequisite for governmental leadership in the church. An elder leader must first be a man proven in spiritual leadership in the home, then in responsibility under other mature leaders, and only then raised to leadership in his own right (I Timothy 3).

One should also note the phenomenon of paranoia in many groups that go astray. This begins with the more mild claim of "they would not be able to understand," but degenerates to the level of "they are out to get us." This begins among the leadership and filters down to the people. This must be distinguished from legitimate guardedness toward the forces of evil. The fear of others from differing communities arises from deep insecurity. A person with such fear cannot engage those who disagree in constructive dialogue. This paranoia was certainly in the Sheepfold leadership and led to their isolationism. We who know the Lord or who are on the cutting edge of a new work of the Spirit need never to fear other basically moral believers. We must not cut ourselves off. Separatism is heresy.

Why did people trust themselves to Sheepfold's weak leadership? It was because the miraculous was supposedly happening. This was a weak criterion for choosing leadership; however, once the choice had been made, the motivation of maintaining the social context of meaningful relationships with others at Sheepfold became very strong.

B. Bitterness and Prophetic Direction

No one who stayed committed to Sheepfold was willing to raise the difficult question of the sources of inspiration. According to Scripture, one may be inspired by self (or the flesh), by evil spirits, and by the Holy Spirit. Therefore, Scripture enjoins us to test the spirits, to prove that which is good (Deut. 13, 18; I John 4:1). We have found that when the hearts of people are not full of love, forgiveness and humility, they are open to deception.

Many of the students of Sheepfold were in a state of bitterness, pride, and unhealed hurt. They were bitter at the legalistic restrictions of fundamentalist backgrounds, bitter toward their parents and bitter toward the administration of the college and its authority and rules. The desire for something new, to break from the past, was great among some. Many were as the proverbial first psychology student who thought he had discovered what was wrong with his parents. Among some, this ushered in an attitude of rebellion to all authority (the college, parents and the Evangelical church).

Scripture also says that rebellion and bitterness lead to false prophecy. These attitudes open the door to evil spirits which can also inspire; the attitudes themselves produce a perspective on life and reality which influences prophecy. Hence, Evangelicalism was seen to be "gangrene." Pastor Tabor was readily influenced by the perspective of the students. **The hearts of people are the second most crucial factor leading to cultic error!** Before they fell into error, their hearts were impure.

This leads us to examine the integral relationship between submitting to true authority and false authority. This relationship exhibits a pattern we have seen over and over again since our experience in Sheepfold, a pattern not usually recognized by writers in these areas.

There are several authority spheres taught in Scripture. They include the authority of the state (government), the family, and the church. The basic boundaries between authority spheres and the limits and extents of authority within each are scripturally derived. We are enjoined to give obedience to the law of the land and its magistrates, but never contrary to Scripture (Acts 5:29; Rom. 13). We are enjoined to submit to church leadership, but never contrary to the Apostolic foundations of teaching or to the detriment of one's conscience and thinking ability (Heb. 13:17). Leaders are exhorted to correct, rebuke, discipline and to set the pattern of organization and responsibility in the church. We must never let cultic authority cause us to shrink from affirming the fact that the Bible sets forth the importance of real authority vested in human beings by God, which authority is to be respected.

Yet in our age, rebellion to authority of all kinds has been rampant. Lawlessness affects both church and society. So it was in the college among evangelical students. The spirit of the 60s rebellion had affected even us! Yet one of the strange but true paradoxes is that when there is rebellion against proper, balanced authority within biblical limits and extents, the person becomes a target for cultic authority and demonic control.

Why is this the case? It is because proper authority, though requiring respect and teachability, never violates the mind or conscience of the individual. Even the Holy Spirit only prompts us and seeks to woo us to willingly obey His promptings. Evil spirits, however, are perfectly willing to place us into a bondage of the will.

We need to understand that pride and the severe bitterness of the heart which leads to rebellion opens one up to demonic influence in the same way that direct occult involvement does! This is why the person who rebels against balanced authority often will submit to a totally controlling cultic authority which seeks the suppression of thinking and conscience. All leadership has clay feet in some regards. Not being willing to submit to imperfect leadership due to pride causes some to look for perfect leadership. Only a pretender can appear to be perfect, and thus delude the proud. For this reason, Rev. Moon is called the "perfect master" by his mesmerized followers.

We have seen these patterns over and over again. Only warfare, prayer and deliverance can free the ones submitted to occult bondage.

How did this pattern fit Sheepfold? Some Sheepfold members were in rebellion against the family, the college, the state and the church. There were anger and bitterness toward what was perceived (sometimes incorrectly and sometimes correctly) as an overstrict narrow upbringing. The churches of the students' backgrounds were also negatively evaluated because of the spirit of cynicism pervasive in the 60s. Whenever we do not appreciate our roots and forgive mistakes and sins, a negative spirit of bitterness takes root in our hearts. This bitter root was manifested directly against the college faculty and **especially** the administration.

The administration, by setting and enforcing college rules, became the surrogate parents in the students' minds. This explains the severe and almost slanderous criticism of the school and Evangelicalism (a gangrene, a cancer eating away true spiritual life). If a teacher was a boring lecturer, he was not described as uninteresting, but as personally spiritually dead, part of the gangrene of death at the school. Spiritual pride took on an air of great superiority.

As the book of Hebrews warns, the root of bitterness can corrupt many. Therefore students without negative reactions took upon themselves such reactions through the influence of their fellows. If new studies led to some uncertainty, it was because Christian liberal arts was wrong, rather than because there was a need to grow and learn more. The spiritual pride of Sheepfold leaders played into the bitter criticisms directed at Evangelicals. Even saintly Chaplain Welsh, who was beloved by all, was looked at in a negative light for he was not yet into the "reality" we had experienced!

People in bitterness, rebellion and pride who open up to the supernatural for revelation speak from the inspiration of their own flesh or from evil spirits. There can indeed be a supernatural dimension beyond coincidence, but this does not prove doctrine. To be under the influence of evil spirits and to have power from them is witchcraft. This is why rebellion is akin to witchcraft; they are intertwined.

Hence, the Sheepfold members who rebelled against proper authority now came under the dominating authority of this particular church. It taught them not to read books, not to think, not to hear other religious teachers, not to judge and read Scripture for themselves, not to further one's education; indeed, it taught them to get all their understanding from Sheepfold Church. Yet Evangelicals were said to be narrow!

Those who intensely rebel **against proper authority** are targets for the Jim Joneses and the more subtle cults with a more decentralized but powerful social-demonic control of members. Humility and love protect us from delusion. Bitterness and rebellion invariably lead to delusion on some level.

Therefore, the second major cause of Sheepfold's destructive direction was that prophetic direction arose from rebellious, bitter or proud hearts which were thereby subject to the influence of evil spirits. This spiritual pride was so intense that it claimed that only we were hearing the Spirit. Yet "testing the spirits" (I John 4) was ignored.

Any church that is not in immorality (exercises discipline) and which preaches the truth is of God. To oppose the church negatively is to oppose the Spirit of God and to fall into dangerous oppression.

C. Scripture as an Objective Revelation

The third **major** or **significant** cause of

the deception at Sheepfold was the **loss of Scripture as an objective revelation**. Scripture is emphatic about the importance of testing future revelation by what has been previously and foundationally established. Deuteronomy 13 emphasized that Israel was not to follow any prophet, even if there were supernatural signs and predictions, if the prophet counseled to forsake biblical teaching concerning God and his relationship to Israel. Many passages can be appealed to for this principle:

1. II Timothy 3:16-17 teaches that the Bible is inspired by God and is the basis for doctrine, correction and instruction in righteousness.
2. Galatians warns of anyone who teaches another gospel other than that laid down by Apostolic teaching (Gal. 1:7-8). Scripture is Apostolic teaching in writing.
3. Apostolic instruction is to be believed and obeyed (II Thes. 3:14-15; I Tim. 6:3-5).

We are especially warned to test the spirits to see if they come from God (I John 4:1). It is significant that the first doctrine undercut at Sheepfold **was this very one** of how to test the spirits. The specific doctrine used here as a test is the incarnation, that Jesus (God the Son) came in the flesh. This is not the only test nor an exhaustive test.

This test was given in response to gnostic teaching that claimed that Jesus only appeared to be human flesh but was not really such. Sheepfold began to question the importance of the historic incarnation and then to interpret this verse to mean Jesus' coming to be formed spiritually in us. This opened the door to full subjectivism in doctrine, since their interpretation of this verse was **the opposite** of the historical contextual meaning. I Thessalonians 5:19-21 gives balanced instruction in regard to prophetic gifts. It says, "Do not put out the Spirit's fire; do not treat prophecies with contempt. **Test everything**. Hold on to the good."

All of this assumed that Scripture provides us with objective revelation for testing all doctrine. Scripture is the plumb line for evaluating further revelation in the Spirit. Scripture must not be subject to reinterpretation according to prophecy and visions or **the objective ground for testing will be lost**. Colossians 2:8 warns against those who take their stand on the basis of dreams and visions and are **puffed up** with idle notions.

How does Scripture become the basis for testing new revelation? It does so through the mind. Passage after passage exhorts us to **think**! The mind is the organ of ability for comparing propositions and discovering contradiction or incoherence. The mind must do its work humbly, without intellectual pride. The mind must recognize the importance of intuitive perception in the realm of Spirit to spirit. Indeed, the mind must submit to Scripture to be renewed in godly thinking (Rom. 12:2). Yet when all is said and done, the mind must apply the laws of logic to test for contradiction.

Watchman Nee brilliantly described the place of the mind in his second volume of **The Spiritual Man**. Although man's inner spirit is the center of receiving intuitive revelation, it is the mind that searches out revelation and expresses it in propositions (meaningful statements). It is the mind which then compares these statements to revelation in Scripture in regard to doctrine and practice. The spiritual mind is indispensable for avoiding error. The laws of logic are part of the equipment of the mind.

Yet at Sheepfold Church the mind was held in suspicion; thinking and logic were in disrepute. Rather than putting to death evil, selfish thinking as part of the old nature, Sheepfold taught the putting to death of the mind itself. The spirit senses and intuits, but the mind comprehends. Having forsaken objective revelation and the mind which evaluates, Sheepfold entered a world in which anything was possible. Their minds evaluated their revelations as true because they seemed to hold together **without objective reference to Scripture**. The mind was still used to evaluate, but it became a darkened mind unenlightened by the Word.

My experience has taught me that a community can be properly open to supernatural experience as long as the place of the *objective Word and testing* remains prominently emphasized. False prophets will eventually show themselves by contradiction to the Word in doctrine or practice. I know of no exception. The office of a prophet is only for the stable mature believer. Even then, we must never forgo testing and prayerful evaluation. Satan is behind false prophecy. If Satan prophesies only truth, he will have no success in his desire to deceive. His method is to capture a group by first giving true prophecy (in accordance with the Word). Later, when the community places its trust in the voice of a person and is caught up in the excitement of the supernatural and has lost its resolve to test prophecies, the devil will speak deception. Even so, people with a gift of discernment sense that "something is off" in the false prophet before anything false has been said.

A sad feature during this period was

the weakness of the Bible faculty of the
college. Just previous to this time, the
college had experienced a mass exodus of
their best professors to a newly expanding
seminary. Some courses in Bible were
taught by men of mediocre qualities. Some
were not men of deep faith, experience nor
inspiring as teachers. Today the college
has recovered and has an excellent faculty.
Yet here is a word for the Christian colleges:
The Bible faculty especially must be staffed
by people of:

1. great faith, experience and love for
   the Lord; personal piety, not just
   intellectual knowledge, is essential;
2. an inspiring classroom ability;
3. solid intellectual ability; and
4. great personal stability of life.

It must be of all faculties the **best** in the
school. Impressionable minds will otherwise conclude that the Bible is less relevant
than other academic subjects or that the
evangelical faith is dry and not where the
life of the Spirit is to be found. Weaknesses
in this regard further spurred the drift
away from solid biblical moorings at
Sheepfold.

It is crucial that the charismatic movement gain a deeper commitment to the
importance of objective biblical scholarship and testing. Allegorical interpretations which play fast and loose with the

meaning of Bible texts out of context must be rejected. The Bible text can be an illustration or a catalyst for another idea not directly taught in the text, but the teacher should never imply that the text itself speaks something other than what is derived from interpretation in its grammatical historical **context**. As has been rightly stated, "A text without context is a pretext."

A knowledge of basic church history might have been a great antidote to the sense of discovering new revelations. The script of Sheepfold Church had been played out before. The libertarian gnostics of the Second and Third centuries, the radical montanists of this period, and the radical charismatics who broke from Scriptural authority and followed Thomas Muntzer during Luther's day are prime examples. For this reason, if for no other, we need to have a more basic knowledge of history in our communities.

In summary, **no believer should ever yield to any group which destroys thinking and the principles of Scripture as an objective revelation and source for testing**.

D. Preoccupation With Miracles

The fourth major area causing spiritual ruin came from Sheepfold's **preoccupation with miracles and power as opposed to**

love. This preoccupation was so great that **miracles of imagination** were spoken of as if they were objectively real. When we examine the miracle accounts of the New Testament we find, in general, that love and compassion motivated Jesus to free people from the bondage of sickness and disease. Yes, the signs and wonders confirmed the preaching of the gospel. Yet signs and wonders were not valued for their own sake or for the heady feeling of power. Rather, the power of love motivated the preaching and **faith and love together in the power of the Spirit produced miracles**. This is a subtle but crucial distinction. A sense of dealing with the supernatural can be very exhilarating. However, this sense can have three sources.

First, the flesh can cause our imagination to run wild. This was the case with the miracles Jerry reported and with the paralyzed little girl. It is true that believers see the hand of God in events that do not prove a direct intervention of God in the natural order. This is legitimate. Yet Sheepfold members claimed stupendous interventions where there were none.

Secondly, the supernatural can be directed by Satan and his hosts. Events certainly occurred which were beyond coincidence. This did not confirm God's **approval**.

Finally, faith and love in the true anointing of God produces miracles. Miracles are not to be sought after for their own sake or for power, but are by-products of other central motives. When we seek power for its own sake, we connect to evil spirits. When we seek love, we connect to God.

E. **Methods Indoctrination**

A fifth explanation of Sheepfold's deception relates to the **methodology of indoctrination**. This was not a planned methodology but was just as effective nonetheless. The slow process of indoctrination and the social influence of peers in the community together formed a powerful motive to adopt Sheepfold's radical reinterpretation of Scripture. Doctrinal aberrations were put forth gradually, withdrawn and reintroduced repeatedly until the community was no longer shocked by the new way of thinking. Thus the changes seemed more minor than they really were. Each stage was only one part of the whole view. Sheepfold provided the center of meaningful relationships for many, there was a strong inducement to remain in the fold.

It is parallel to the young person in high school who has heard of the dangers of lung cancer. His peers urge him to try "just one puff" of a cigarette. "One puff can't hurt you," they say. Next he is encouraged to have a whole cigarette. Before long, he is a smoker.

So at Sheepfold it was "just take a puff" of radical doctrine. "It's only a small change; it can't hurt that much, so why not?" Then a whole new doctrine was inhaled. Eventually, a whole new theology was adopted using some biblical language, but diametrically opposed to biblical teaching.

We can call this phenomenon gradualism and the influence of strong social pressure from peer groups. Gradualism is the "boiling the frog" phenomenon described earlier. The combination of gradualism and peer pressure is a major influence causing many to succumb to cults.

F. Isolationism

A sixth important component in Sheepfold's demise was the **decision for isolation**. No one was allowed to speak into the life of the congregation from the outside. It was said, "They wouldn't understand." We never outgrow our need to be teachable, to learn from others and to be accountable to others. Yet, **in pride** they cut off their relationships with other charismatic and non-charismatic leaders. This is a major mark of cultic direction in a group. An inability to hear from others is the mark of insecurity which seeks to shield itself from any criticism. The claim that others would not be able to understand expanded to the point that only "the initiated" could be admitted to secret revelation. Against this gnostic claim of secret mysteries, the New Testament gospel is a revelation of depth that is proclaimed openly to all. The first two chapters of Colossians and Ephesians were written to counter the argument of those who held to a secret-mystery view of revelation.

In summary, we wish to note that Sheepfold Church both follows and breaks the mold of what is usually seen as the path to cultic bondage:

- There was no strong cultic leader who personally dominated the lives of his followers.
- There were no blatant brainwashing techniques such as long hours of lectures, lack of sleep and "love-bombing" (surrounding the person with love, hugs and words of encouragement in the midst of a long, sleepless regimen).

Yet the method of gradualism and social influence was just as effective in producing conformity.

Other dimensions were certainly parallel to the cults. These were:

- twisting of biblical passages (called Bible-bending by Jim Sire),

- social pressures to accept prevailing radical views, and
- the denial of key orthodox doctrines.

Yet what is so important about Sheepfold is *where* it did not conform to the cults, the subtlety of its early errors. Today's danger often comes from groups which appear on the surface to be acceptable. However, whenever a group allows bitterness and rebellion to become important motives in congregational direction, Satan can begin to control and direct the life of that congregation and the people in it. Once Satan has control over a group he can, through his hosts of hell, supernaturally act to use this group for his ends. No strong leader is necessary.

Mature, stable leadership is the safeguard against the wiles of the devil. Proper authority on the basis of Scripture is an antidote to error. Sadly we have had personal contact with communities in recent times whose development amazingly parallels Sheepfold.

In summary, we list those marks and danger signs reflected at Sheepfold Church. Use them to aid in your own discernment:

1. Roots of bitterness in a significant segment of people who are giving direction in the congregation, including:

   a. prophecy motivated by pride and

rebellion,

b. rebellion against proper authority in congregational members' lives/rejection of biblically ordered groups.

2. Spiritual pride: "We are better than others."

3. The rejection of Scripture as an *objective revelation* for testing all teaching and prophecy; e.g., spiritualizing or allegorizing Scripture.

4. Disparaging the proper place of the mind and thinking in testing doctrine; e.g., the mind must be crucified; a radical division between mind and spirit.

5. Neglect of the lessons of history.

6. A desire for miraculous power without the desire for love and service.

7. A subtle methodology of slow indoctrination—putting forth and withdrawing radical viewpoints.

8. A strong social influence to accept prevailing views.

9. Isolation from other leaders and groups.

10. Revelation seen as a secret mystery only the initiated can understand.

11. Supernatural phenomena without Scriptural evaluation.

12. Untested immature leadership not fitting the standards of I Tim. 3.

A Note
On Women
In Leadership

I would not be true to my own convictions if in dealing with the issue of
deception, I did not speak of the issue of
women in leadership. It is my conviction,
despite much debate among Evangelicals,
that God has established a distinction of
roles for men and women and that this distinction of roles is to be reflected both in the
family and the congregation. One of the
sources of community deception is often to
be found in women assuming roles that are
not proper both in the home and the church.
Another such source of deception is men in
leadership representing a home that is not
in right spiritual order according to I Tim. 3.

Having said all concerning mutual submission, love and selflessness, Ephesians
five clearly teaches that the husband has
authority in the home. The general is not
better than the corporal, but he has greater
authority. So the husband is called to imi-
tate the Messiah in his authority in the
home. The proper, loving exercise of this
authority in an orderly home is a key criteria for eldership in I Tim. 3. The structure of
authority in the church therefore is built

upon the structure of the home. It enhances, complements and reflects the home. To reverse authority in the church whereby the wife would be an elder over her husband would have been unthinkable to the apostles.

Is there a reason for this role distinction beyond the value of teaching children to learn from role distinctions in their authority relationships? Yes, there is, and it is connected with the issue of deception. A man who rules his home well is less likely to fall to deception. He is secure as an individual. I Timothy 2:11-14 gives a further reason connected to deception. This passage is often misunderstood. Paul is teaching that a woman should not teach or have authority over a man. I take this to mean teaching in contexts and content which would give her governmental authority over men. Paul then gives us his reason, the structure of the creation order. Adam was formed, then Eve. In the Genesis account this is expanded to show that Eve was given to Adam as his helper and partner. Authority vested in the man is as old as creation. It is not a result of the fall, although the wrong exercise of that authority is a result of the fall. Finally, Paul argues, the woman was first deceived. What is the point of this being included in the argument? Women, called the weaker vessel in

Scripture, are weaker only in some regards.
She is first deceived because of this weakness. Here Paul is speaking of a general
principle, not true of each and every woman.
It is woman's greater sensitivity to the
intuitive and spiritual. Hence we find that
Satan chooses to tempt through the woman.
Women in general are more sensitive to
spiritual things; they make up a larger per-
centage of most congregations. Yet this
sensitivity predisposes them to spiritual
influences both good and evil. Men, with
more of a tendency to question, are often
slower to receive spiritual promptings, but
less apt to fall into deception. Hence,
governmental authority and protection for
the flock is given to men who prove themselves in family leadership. Does this mean
that men may not be as spiritually sensitive and deceived at times? No, it does not.
Nor does it mean that a woman may not
develop a high ability of testing. It simply
means that the tendency in general of the
sexes is to be reflected positively in roles
and in the training of men and women for
their respective roles in the home and the
church. This works against the dangers of
deception although it does not preclude it.
Men proven in their families, scripturally
trained, and who love the flock are a bulwark against deception.

Afterward

III. AFTERWARD

After leaving Sheepfold Church we were turned off to the claims of the charismatic movement. For a time, my wife and I became Evangelical rationalists. I believed in God and that He ordered my existence. Yet guidance in life only came by applying ethical standards and empirical-rational considerations to circumstances. I radically held that the Holy Spirit never revealed Himself. If someone came to the rational conclusion that Jesus was Lord, the Holy Spirit was involved in this, but imperceptibly. The Holy Spirit only pointed to Jesus, and this Jesus was the historical Jesus and the Jesus in heaven, not the present experience of Jesus.

Patty and I attended an Evangelical Lutheran church and found healing in the hymns, the liturgy and the Lord's Supper. Yes, God was real, but I was running from the irrational subjectivism I called "charismania." People on opposite poles said, "Thus saith the Lord"; I had had enough of that! As yet I didn't understand the intuitive spiritual side of man's being nor the workings of the devil.

After two years of graduate school, two years of seminary and thirteen years in the pastorate, I have come to some clear, hopefully more balanced conclusions. I want to share my progression of experiences with you. Perhaps it will be helpful.

The study of Scripture convinced me that the supernatural gifts of the Holy Spirit were not just for one age. Mark 16:17, even if not in the original text, is a clear summary of what the early church believed. The New Testament speaks of spiritual manifestations, miracles, and the gifts of the Spirit as a normal part of church life. The supernatural intervention of God manifested His reality, and confirmed his communication from Genesis to Revelation. I simply could not be convinced against the gifts of the Spirit by current arguments that they were only needed to establish the early church before the written word was given (Warfield, **Counterfeit Miracles**), or that they were for another dispensation. If these gifts were valid then, why not now when unbelief, secularism and occultism are great indeed?

Secondly, I knew of both miracles and manifestations I simply could not discount. There was my Lutheran friend Tom who was supernaturally healed after a car accident. There was Eugene, healed of a club foot. Likewise, men of God, who did not identify themselves as charismatics or pentecostals, certainly had spiritual gifts.

V. Raymond Edman of Wheaton exhibited supernatural words of wisdom and knowledge, and had many supernatural experiences. Chaplain Evan Welsh exhibited gifts as well. I, therefore, concluded that the gifts were real today. They are present among Christians, but often unrecognized because they are unnamed. I was, as yet, unconvinced that the gifts of the Spirit were more especially manifest among charismatics who perhaps were deluded by wishful thinking.

With this viewpoint, I entered the Presbyterian ministry and pastored my first congregation. At this time I also concluded that every believer had the "baptism in the Spirit" at conversion and that speaking in tongues (the ability I little used) was not a prerequisite to other gifts. I did not yet know of a community that was really practicing the gifts of the Spirit in love and power. Therefore, my ministry was a rational effort type ministry.

Soon after entering the pastorate, two of our members put me in touch with Reba Place Fellowship in Chicago. Fania had a sister in this community, Vera, who invited us for hospitality. Later we attended their services. In those days Reba was a total sharing Christian community. Reba was my first indepth experience with a charismatic community in Scriptural balance.

They did not teach tongues as the necessary sign of the "the baptism." However, they manifested prophecy, healing, tongues, interpretation and other spiritual gifts as part of their corporate and individual lives. There was mature leadership on a firm basis of biblical authority, a leadership concerned and committed enough to test the spirits.

It was marvelous. Wonderful worship combined modern and classical elements. There was love, truth, beauty and goodness. Yes, the charismatic dimension was real and could exist in balance. The fruit in people's lives, the reality of words of wisdom and the prophetic gifts proved true.

My second great step back to the charismatic world came in experiencing the world of spiritual oppression and the need to free others by deliverance-prayer. I found that people who were unable to gain release in psychiatry or mundane forms of counseling were freed after renunciation and prayer commanding the bonds of Satan to be broken (see K. Koch's many works; M. Bubeck, **The Adversary**). Amazingly, in tough counseling situations I intuitively received the supernatural discernment of spirits to enable me to help others. At times I knew the problem even before words were even exchanged with a new counselee. There was prayer for healing which showed great results, although perhaps not of a totally provable character for apologetic purposes. Yet probable evidence was there. Since that time we have seen predictive prophecy fulfilled and healing of a more supernatural character.

Yet, I also knew that my non-charismatic (not anti) professors were men of piety. At times they literally loved their lessons into us, combining a depth of scholarship with faith and love. I could not reject the values of study nor the reality of the charismatic dimension. I could not reject the Evangelicals nor the Charismatics. Both had given me so much.

Today I lead a frankly charismatic congregation (manifesting the gifts of the Spirit). Yet I know and love the Spirit in my brethren of Presbyterian, Baptist and other backgrounds. I needed to think out a new biblical approach to the whole subject. Amazingly, great books came to my attention which helped in the search.

The mind of man cannot seem to avoid confronting opposing views, and factions will arise. Words both reveal and hide reality. However, a humble searching spirit has the opportunity to transcend limited perspectives to achieve a more adequate viewpoint. One of the discoveries during these years was that of the nineteenth century revivalists.

There was a broad consensus among many giants of faith from different denominational backgrounds. Charles Finney, D.L. Moody, R.A. Torrey, and Andrew Murray all spoke of the reality of the gifts of the Spirit and the "baptism in the Spirit." Murray wrote a book on healing and gained great insight into spiritual gifts. None spoke of tongues as a "sine qua non" sign of the baptism in the Spirit or as a necessary prerequisite to other spiritual gifts. Was it possible that the Pentecostal movement, despite its gain in understanding spiritual gifts and manifesting the power of God, was the carrier as well of unnecessary division in the Body of the Messiah? Was it also possible that the fundamentalists formed their doctrine in reaction rather than in humble searching, and thereby created further division?

One thing is clear: powerful supernatural spiritual gifts flowed in these nineteenth century leaders and they did not dot their i's and cross their t's like either modern Pentecostalism nor Fundamentalism. Is there a theological key?

I believe there is indeed a key. Scripture is clear that upon accepting the Messiah Jesus into our lives, we have by grace been given all things in Him. We have died with Him, risen in Him, have been made partakers of His Spirit and have ascended to the heavenlies in Him. In Him, we have all.

Yet this refers to our positional standing. Theologians have long made a distinction between the positional reality of our identity in the Messiah and our practical appropriation in living out the truths of our position.

Watchman Nee wrote of the dramatic change that came with his understanding of his co-death with the Messiah. When he entered into the **full experience** of this reality he shouted, "I'm dead! Praise God!" Yet this was true before his realization. Indeed, the "baptism in the Spirit" could be of a similar nature. As His born-again followers, we are already **in Him**, "baptized in the Spirit." Yet it is not until later that most come into the practical experience or reality of the meaning of the baptism. By faith it is appropriated.

Evangelicals and Charismatics disagree over whether or not the "baptism in the Spirit" occurs at conversion or in a "second blessing" experience. Parallel to the reality of our co-death with the Messiah, the answer is surely both! The experience of what is ours in the Messiah is new **to us**. The baptism **positionally** takes place at conversion. It is **appropriated** subsequently any time from minutes to years afterward, when we experience a faith-understanding and we finally take hold of what is ours.

Spiritual gifts are manifestations of this baptism. Tongues is the easiest spiritual gift to manifest, therefore tongues often accompanies the practical appropriation of the "baptism in the Spirit." However, this is not always so, nor can it be **demonstrated** from Scripture. It is rather an inference from the fact of tongues accompanying the gift of the Holy Spirit in four passages in the book of Acts (Acts 2, 8, 10, 19).

We can see how the split is fostered, for some Evangelicals argue that the "baptism in the Holy Spirit" is in **every sense** an accompaniment of conversion and that the gifts of the Spirit were for another age.

I began to see this as **the devil's bifurcation**. It produced two wings of the church which greatly needed each other. One wing emphasized the objective rational interpretation of Scripture. They possessed the majority of believing biblical scholars. The other wing produced the intuitive, spiritually sensitive, experientially oriented leaders. Yet in the 19th century the two emphases came together even in single individuals.

In recent decades we have seen an Evangelicalism grow that is scholastic and intellectualistic, and a Pentecostalism which is subjectivistic as each hardened positions in reaction to the other. The anti-intellectual spiritual opposed the pro-intellectual anti-experiential. Yet the only thing that can bring balance is the reality of the Wind of the Spirit combined with the discipline of clear thinking in handling Holy Writ.

Today, praise God, this false dichotomy is breaking down. A pentecostal scholar, Robert Cooley, leads one of our finest seminaries (Gordon-Conwell) and Pentecostals or charismatics are found on such faculties as Trinity and Fuller. A great Evangelical scholar, Clark Pinnock, invites fellow Evangelicals to **enter in** to the experience of the Holy Spirit and His gifts and to learn from charismatics. Many emphasize testing the spirits and that fruit is more important than gifts.

In many ways Sheepfold Church was a tragedy born of the false division in the church. The church needs to present its young people with **the reality of the experience of piety** in prayer, the gifts of the Spirit and the miracles that manifest themselves in the Wind of the Spirit, as well as the importance of hard biblical thinking. In any unbiased reading of the New Testament, it becomes evident that a walk in the power of the Holy Spirit produces miraculous manifestations of answered prayer, healing and supernatural gifts. This was true for a host of saintly leaders including Charles Finney, R.A. Torrey, Andrew Murray, D.L. Moody, Rees Howells, Hudson Taylor, G. Mueller, C.T. Studd, V. Raymond Edman, and many others.

The objective revelation of the Scripture for doctrine and correction, and the importance of humble, patient biblical scholars should be stressed. Without them we would be bereft of English translations, grammatical tools, lexicons, dictionaries and encyclopedias. Respect for the Word and handling it carefully produces respect for the humble, pious thinker and scholar.

The Evangelicals need to open up and **enter in** by faith to the fresh word of God's Spirit and His gifts, while the charismatic needs greater concern for objective interpretation. We need to come together. Neither a cold rationalism nor an interpretive subjectivism will be adequate for a day of great spiritual deceptions by the Prince of Darkness. Let us not argue over words. Let us enter into the reality of spiritual life tested by the Word.

This leads to some comments concerning the dangers of Christian college educations. We certainly cannot blame the college for losing its best biblical teachers to a new and expanding seminary. Yet, it proves something crucial about the Bible and Theology college faculty. Its members must be superb in knowledge and **inspired** in teaching. They must not only have head knowledge, but be mature in spiritual experience. They serve as key models for students; their lives require elder-level maturity as in I Tim. 3.

Teachers convey not only their head knowledge, but their lives. One of the reasons by God's grace that I was able to resist the spiritual disease of Sheepfold was that I found such teachers! The biblical faculty therefore must reflect the greatest excellence so students will not make false judgments about the Bible's relevance based on an uninspiring faculty.

However, the rest of the faculty needs to integrate all areas of knowledge from a firm biblical base. It simply will not do to teach secular psychology, literature, science. Integration and Scriptural evaluation need to come from faculty members who also reflect a deep maturity of spiritual life and experience. The students must not simply be tossed into the deep waters of the intellectual world and told to swim. Some will swim, but too many will drown. Christian education, as secular education, can produce tremendous doubt and destruction if not **carefully handled**.

I have also become certain that one of

the dangers to the believing student is to be wrenched out of his home church and to be transplanted hundreds or thousands of miles away to a college that for many replaces the church. Relationship to the local church is not like membership in a lecture club where one can transfer to any city and find the same lectures. Scripture teaches that a church relationship is like an extended family in which the members are responsible for one another for nurture and encouragement. Therefore we would question whether the Christian college can replace the student's church for four years.

Of course the college urges church attendance, but many on campus drop out since they have daily chapel and relationships with believing students. A student needs seriously to consider staying in his home church and building his life around this. If God leads him to a distant school, he should find a good congregation and be intimately involved as his first priority. There is reason to question the societal pattern of wrenching 17- and 18-year-olds away from a family social context in the most crucial transition period of their lives. There are enough Christian schools today that this should not be necessary.

Secondly, the Christian college should deemphasize chapel (although I have nothing against having even required chapel). The requirement of church attendance and service is more biblically sensible. The student needs the nurture of the **church family**. If other students and faculty attend, he will find both fellowship and commonality within the church. After all, if the college is really Christian it can expect its constituents to live as Christians, which naturally implies being a **significant** part of a church. The church needs to provide substantial ministry to students even if they may be only four-year members.

I believe that weaknesses in each of these areas contributed to the Sheepfold phenomenon. However, I am delighted to say that I see great strides in Christian colleges toward correcting these deficiencies.

Most crucially, pastors and teachers need to unflaggingly encourage young people in the spiritual disciplines of prayer, worship and meditative Bible reading. This is more important than any other discipline. They must not assume a student can apply himself to these disciplines just because he comes from a Christian background.

In summary, I want to plead for Evangelicals and charismatics to get together and find a way out of this doctrinal impasse. Their valid perspectives can be integrated. This is so desperately needed. Secondly, I want to urge that Christian colleges and the churches together find better ways to integrate their ministries and more creatively foster the spiritual growth of their students.

The
Issue of
Authority

IV. THE ISSUE OF AUTHORITY

Sheepfold Church reflected an age in rebellion to authority. Perhaps the experience of Sheepfold motivated me to search into the issue of authority. We live in an age of many "self-proclaimed Messiahs." All around us are men who do not come with credentials of affirmation from others to whom they are truly accountable. They set themselves up as authorities. In my view, Scripture teaches that we deeply need one another to speak into each other's lives. We never outgrow our need for the accountability that comes from relationships. Pastors need one another; leaders need one another. Sheep need shepherds.

Today the church is beset by the extremes of both authoritarianism and congregational anarchy. Balanced authority in the church is one of the great safeguards against destructive tendencies.

What is the nature of true authority? Authority in the church is, of course, based on the Written Word. All are responsible to understand the basics of Scripture and not to follow directions or doctrines contrary to the Word. All authority in the church is under the Authority of Jesus. Yet after making allowance for the supremacy of the Word and the fact that Scripture primarily calls us to a servanthood—not a position— we must admit that Scripture gives servant-leaders authority in the church.

Servant-leaders are those who prove themselves by humility, the fruit of the Spirit, solid knowledge of the Word, and a loving care for the people of God. Servant-leaders prove themselves first by being in submission to authority. When servant-leaders are chosen of God, Scripture gives to them the role of governing in the congregations of the Messiah. They are enjoined to shepherd the flock (I Peter 5), to teach, to admonish, to correct and to discipline. Scripture enjoins the flock to submit to their leadership (Heb. 13:17). This submission **never means the forfeiture of our own minds or consciences**. Nor does it mean that members of the flock cannot in an edifying way voice their disagreement. Yet ultimately the leaders set direction for the congregation. Submission implies:

1. Pulling together in unity and prayer with the direction leadership sets as long as it is not contrary to Scripture or conscience. Elder leadership also has authority to install and remove people from lesser positions.
2. Being willing to be taught and counseled by leadership; maintaining a

humble and teachable attitude. Discipleship includes following the pattern of mature leaders to the degree that their pattern reflects Jesus.

3. Reserving the right of final personal decisions for oneself, though given to counsel with real listening and searching. Everyone must ultimately stand in his own conscience before God.

Leaders need to submit to a *plurality of other leaders*. Authority in the New Testament is vested in a mutually accountable **plural** leadership though there may be a head pastor. Furthermore, we must beware of the isolated group that cuts itself off from other groups. We need brothers and sisters outside of our limited circle to interact with our lives. There is only one church of God; we must see all elders as fellow leaders in the same universal body.

Biblical leadership is given the authority to discipline in regard to sin and serious error. This discipline begins with words of loving exhortation and correction which seeks reconciliation with the offending brother. However, if repentance is not forthcoming, it can lead to the painful discipline of disfellowshipping or excommunication. This is to turn the brother who is in gross sin (I Cor. 5:11-13) back to God as well as to protect the purity of the church. Especially, the church must guard against bitterness, slander and rebellion in its membership. These are the roots of false prophecy. Lack of discipline in many quarters in the church is a great danger. The church needs to study thoroughly what Scripture says on government, authority and discipline. One of the sad aspects of Sheepfold was that no decision of discipline for immorality or heresy was ever given against Sheepfold by the rest of the church, or in regard to individual members and faculty.

Unfortunately, one of the great problems of our day is acting out of reaction. The Devil's **tactic** is clear. Whenever proper biblical discipline and authority is invoked, cries of "Jonestown" and "Shepherding movement" resound. The Devil's method is to use the extremes of cultic authority and authoritarianism to produce popular outcries which reduce leadership to impotence. Leaders give up their God-given call to hear from God, to set direction and to teach and discipline, and to thereby protect the flock. Instead they become public relations experts seeking to find ways to please all the varying sentiments of the membership. This fear on the part of leaders produces a weak church with poorly trained and discipled members who are pawns for aberrant movements.

Of this I am now sure: proper Biblical

authority is a bulwark against cultism and false controlling authorities. Over and over again I have seen those who rebel against proper authority become fully subject to false cultic authority. This is because rebellion, akin to witchcraft, is spiritually capable of being controlled by the devil. The solution for false cultic authority is not the anarchy of the absence of authority. It is rather a return to a biblical teaching on the nature and place of authority and insisting on it in our congregations.

Wild accusations against the excesses in some parts of the "shepherding movement," claims that we are in danger of "shepherding," and overreactions to the cults produce fear of proper authority. **Unproven accusations** produce a reactive stance and divert us from **deeply studying the biblical passages that deal with the issues of conforming our lives and church patterns to the Word**. Thus the Devil produces in the church exactly what he desires: either false cultic authority or an anarchistic lack of authority. As people react in bitterness and slander, the Prince of the Air gains victories. Let us not carry bad reports against any group unless a Matthew 18 process of discipline and evidence has been clearly followed. False movements are handled by church authority and decision, not by its absence.

What is the nature of authority? True authority seeks as its goal the maturity of the Messiah in every individual. It seeks to facilitate in people the ability to know the Word, to pray effectively, and to manifest the gifts and fruit of the Spirit. **It seeks to produce strong individuals in the Lord who are capable of spiritual discernment and solid thinking!** True submission is not dependency, but is coordinate with the strongest self-confidence and character.

False authority seeks to make people dependent on the authority. It seeks to discern and think for other people, suppressing their conscience and thinking. **The goals of true and false authority are therefore opposite and determine the patterns which are worked out in the life of the congregation.**

All men and women are forever fallible. Practical perfection, though the goal of our lives, is not to be obtained in this life. One of the pitfalls of the proud is an inability to maintain congregational commitment because servant-leaders are not deemed perfect enough. This is a dangerous stance. We can learn from anyone who loves the Lord. We can accept that God is working through any servant-leader who demonstrates a love for worshiping God, a love for the Word, and whose family life is in basic order according to I Tim. 3. A servant-leader who shows imperfection is far to be preferred over one who has learned in pretense to project an image beyond his spiritual attainment.

All of us are called to submit to imperfect leaders (with clay feet). Those who admit their faults and pray for one another are to be more greatly esteemed. The quest of pride for perfect leadership, or the complaint that leaders are not (adequately) worthy of respect—even though they fulfill basic biblical criteria—is a danger signal. Such a person also may find himself attracted to a cultic leader who is full of lies and deception but has learned to **project** the image of perfection.

God has called us all to build His kingdom. In its present form, His church is not yet perfected. We are called to live and act in love and compassionate tolerance for the benefit of all in His kingdom. With new measures of love and spiritual anointing, we are called to a task of listening and learning. Let us recognize in these "last days" that the Devil "goes about as a roaring lion, seeking whom he may devour." Unless we draw together, seek to find Biblical grounds for greater accord in a spirit of humility, and unless we cease to build doctrine from reaction, the devil will have an easy time. If oppression and persecution come, the foundations must be firm and loyalty must be instilled in the troops.

The Sheepfold Church phenomenon touches many with the key issues of the church today. These issues include the charismatic/non-charismatic debate, models of authority, the nature of cultic control and rebellion, the symptoms of would-be heretical groups and false authoritarianism, the educational structure for raising our children as mature, spiritual and knowledgeable believers, and the authority of Scripture as an objective revelation. It is our prayer that the lessons to be learned from Sheepfold will shed light on these issues and give direction to those in confusion.

Helping
The
Wounded

V. HELPING THE WOUNDED

Although Scripture makes it abundantly clear that leaders bear a higher responsibility and punishment for leading people into deception, the follower still has a responsibility as well.

The major issue in healing these wounded individuals is finding the roots of why the person gave himself to the deception. Our experience in providing such healing has proved to us that there is no such thing as a person being innocently deceived. The Scriptures promise that the followers of Jesus (His sheep) hear His voice, know Him, and follow Him.

The roots of deception are always in pride and bitterness (unhealed hurt). This is a problem all face; therefore, all are capable of being deceived. The healing process is as follows.

First, on the subject of pride, let me put forth the following. Pride is the root that causes people to buy into deceptions that they are part of *the key group being used by God*, or are **part of the group that possesses the truth in a way that is beyond all others.** This produces a heady feeling that can be mistaken for the Spirit. If this is identified as the key, then the person needs to repent of pride and admit this fault.

Secondly, on the subject of unhealed hurts, it is important to note that unhealed hurt is bitterness. Many say, "I am not bitter, only hurt." Hurt turns to bitterness very quickly. The cure for unhealed hurt is in identifying with the death of Jesus on the cross (envisioning it, meditating on the truth of it, etc.) and coming to the place where the person can truly say of those who hurt him, "Father, forgive them, for they know not what they do." Forgiveness in this sense may not mean the restoration of the relationship; that requires the guilty to repent and restore. However, it is a commitment to have love for the offender and to pray for his repentance and restoration to blessing. The roots of unhealed hurt are usually in the closest relationships (parents, siblings, teachers, and friends). When the wounded believer has left the cultic group, his primary bitterness will be focused on the leadership of the group. However, this usually is not the root of the problem. The person needs to see the deeper roots and confess them. Then forgiveness toward the cult leaders can follow. (Forgiveness in this sense does not mean letting them off the hook of God's righteousness or not pursuing His justice in love).

The knowledge of the Word is a safeguard against deception. However, the deceived often will not honestly search the Scriptures. I have seen well-taught believers fall into deception. I have also seen new, naive believers recognize that something is wrong with a leader or group. They seek the truth in Scripture and the counsel of others, and God gives them clarity concerning the situation.

After confessing and receiving forgiveness, spiritual deliverance may bo crucial. It is at least well to command any occult or other spirits of deception to be gone.

After this the person requires a period of time to build trust in true elders and deacons. The standards for leaders should be taught to the person. A Biblically balanced knowledge of true authority and submission should be taught. Those from difficult backgrounds often trust people they shouldn't, and refuse to trust those they should. Discipling in the Word where there is weakness and learning how and who to trust is very important.

There are many good healing resources for the unhealed hurt. There are also materials of poor quality. As a start, I would recommend Leanne Payne's *The Healing Presence.* Developing open relationships in a solid, Bible-based community is the capstone of healing. Sometimes the person in the healing process wants to flee. Much prayer and love is sometimes needed. However, we have seen many restored to wholeness.

The
Spirit of
American
Religious Life

VI. THE SPIRIT OF
AMERICAN RELIGIOUS LIFE

I believe that we live in perilous times, even as this chapter is being written. Thus, there are several reasons for why the lessons of *Dynamics* are so important for today. I write this after the recent tragedy of the Branch Davidians in Waco, Texas, who were destroyed in an explosive fire after many weeks of siege by federal agents. This cult showed how far deception can go.

First is the condition of our population. With the decline of educational standards and the media's influence in building public consensus, we are in for great dangers. The Canadian philosopher Marshall McLuwen called media influence "cold communication." Truth questions are not asked. People do not know how to think. What is seen is taken as truth. The experience is all that counts. This trend is found as well in the media orientation of some mega-congregations and in television ministries. The claims and doctrine are not subject to scrutiny because, in my perception, gullibility in the Christian public is at an alarming level. This is producing a shallow, media-type spirituality. It is short on real Biblical content (keep those messages entertaining and down to 15 minutes), and very large on hype.

The second grave danger is the teaching that has come out of some large charismatic ministries defending the non-accountability of the head leader. He is compared to the King of Israel or to the High Priest. It is argued that he is accountable only to God. To seek to bring discipline to him through due process, as in Matthew 18, is said to be a violation of the principle to not touch God's anointed. Many such circles do not hold to I Timothy 3 standards for leaders. This is a dangerous situation that can lead to great disillusionment and destruction.

The third danger is the continued growth of New Age spirituality. The ultimate prophetic direction of Sheepfold was New Age. Granted, there are people and movements who minister prophetically being falsely accused of New Age tendencies because they pray for emotional healing and have visions. However, the number of New Agers who have significant demonic and occult abilities have increased, and they can deceive believers if they infiltrate into charismatic circles. Discernment in the Spirit and rigor in Biblical testing for all teaching are safeguards. However, this testing must be done without a critical or paranoid spirit, which can also lead to deception. We must trust the Lord to guard His people from deception because they walk before Him in humility and forgiveness.

One of the keys to avoiding the deceptions that arise from these dangers is utilizing a quality discipleship program through small groups overseen by truly accountable and healthy leaders. The elders can be accountable to each other and to leaders outside of the local structure. It is important for congregations to not be sectarian in separateness from others. People need to ask serious questions about accountability, doctrine, and structure. (Our book *Due Process* deals with many of these issues.) Discipleship must deal with character building in the context of solid Biblical teaching. Character is built in service. Actually, those who are prone to deception will likely be deceived and those prone to lead in unhealthy ways will likely do so. What is the solution? It is for those who see the issues and who are spiritually healthy to raise up disciples so more and more of the people of God will be healthy. Healthy believers of character, true doctrine, and spiritual anointing will not be prone to deception.

Tikkun Ministries

Tikkun is a Hebrew term that means **restoration**. It reflects our burden and belief. We believe Scripture teaches that the Church will be restored to power, love, unity and righteousness. This renewal will be a key to the restoration of the Jewish people and their ingrafting into **"her own olive tree"** (Romans 11). We believe that the last days, according to Scripture, will see a progression of events leading toward the full restoration of Israel and the Church. As the Church is restored, we will see a significant number of Jews saved and a continued return of Jews to Israel. With those Jews who are the saved remnant of Israel, the Church will intercede and witness in love until Israel turns to Yeshua. Romans 11 is a key passage of last days teaching. Tikkun Ministries is committed to seeing these restorations come to pass in the last days.

As part of our vision we are engaged in the following ministries:

1. Training, sending out and supporting congregational planters in the United States, Israel and other countries.
2. Fostering Jewish ministry in local churches.
3. A full-time Bible and graduate School for training leaders for the Jewish vineyard and for work in the Church.

4. Sending out teachers and preachers for conferences, evangelistic campaigns, services in Messianic congregations and churches, etc.
5. Sponsoring music and dance ministries.
6. Helping to bring about a consistent pattern of unity with the Body as an expression of our deep conviction.

If you are interested in further information on Tikkun Ministries, or if you would like to have someone speak for a conference, seminar or Church service, please phone (301) 977-0156.

The following pages list books available by our Tikkun leaders. Please use the form at the back of this book to place your order.

LAST DAYS TRILOGY

ISRAEL, THE CHURCH AND THE LAST DAYS
Must reading for all believers who want an exciting new perspective on the last days and the end-time role of Israel and the Church.
Price $9.95

FROM IRAQ TO ARMAGEDDON
This book gives an in-depth analysis of end-time prophecy concerning the Middle East.
Price $7.95

REVELATION: THE PASSOVER KEY
An intriguing analysis explaining the similarities of the exodus from Egypt to the end times.
Price $6.95

MESSIANIC JEWISH THEMES

Jewish Roots, A Foundation of Biblical Theology
A significant book on Messianic Judaism which offers insight on many difficult questions. $10.00

Growing to Maturity, A Messianic Jewish Guide
This book is used by many congregations for membership classes. $9.00

Jewishness and Jesus
A booklet to help you share Messiah with your unsaved Jewish friends. $1.00

OTHER BOOKS BY OUR AUTHORS

Keith Intrater

The Apple of His Eye
Find out how your life can be transformed as you are bathed in the light of God's grace. $6.00

Covenant Relationships
A handbook on the biblical principles of integrity and loyalty. This book lays

important foundations for congregational health and right spiritual attitudes. $12.00

Dan Juster

Dynamics of Spiritual Deception

This book will help you to avoid demonic counterfeit in Spirit-filled congregations. $5.95

Due Process

This book reveals the need for God's people to pursue, in love, godly justice. $6.95

LD101	Israel, the Church and the Last Days	$9.95
LD102	From Iraq to Armageddon...........................	7.95
LD103	Revelation: The Passover Key....................	6.95
MJ201	Jewish Roots...	10.00
MJ202	Growing to Maturity	9.00
MJ203	Jewishness and Jesus.................................	1.00
AM304	The Apple of His Eye	6.00
AM305	Covenant Relationships..............................	12.00
AM306	Dynamics of Spiritual Deception..............	5.95
AM307	Duo Prooooo..	6.95

Name_____Phone_____
Address_____
_____

All items available to ministries and bookstores, in quantities of 5 or more, at 40% discount.

Please turn to following order form and fill out the complete information for each book order:

1. The item number

2. The cost of the book

3. The number of that item you would like to order

4. The amount of each item

5. The totals and the amount enclosed.

ITEM	COST/BOOK	NO. ORDERED	AMOUNT
		Subtotal	
Maryland residents add 5% Sales Tax			
(or send tax exempt certificate for our files)			
		15% P & H	
		($2.00 minimum)	
	TOTAL ENCLOSED		

Mail all orders with checks payable to:

Tikkun Ministries
13-15 E. Deer Park Drive, Suite 202
Gaithersburg, MD 20877